LOSE WEIGHT! GET LAID! FIND GOD!

Legal disclaimer: Following this book improves your chances of leading an eventful and rewarding life, but the authors make no legally binding representations or warranties as to its effect. Neither the publisher nor the authors shall be liable for any ruined, misspent or wasted lives, nor indeed for any early loss of life, whether directly or indirectly attributable to this book.

BENRIK LIMITED

Benrik are Ben Carey and Henrik Delehag, the London-based authors of the cult bestselling "This Book Will Change Your Life" series. With over 300,000 copies sold worldwide, it has changed countless lives, although not necessarily for the better. Benrik's cult of "extreme self-improvement" aims to introduce an element of welcome anarchy into people's existence.

Their corporate message is pithy: "Your values are our toilet paper."
Their followers gather like moths to a flame on their aptly-named site www.thiswebsitewillchangeyourlife.com, where you may fill in a form to include them in your will when you pass on. Thank you very much.

Life is short, so make the most of it by planning ahead.
Lose Weight! Get Laid! Find God!
contains all the essential stages of life, one year at a time, so you don't skip any by mistake. It also contains exclusive full-color tips that will ensure each year of your existence makes a lasting impression. You can join the life-planning program at any point: even if your life is well under way, you can tick off the stages you've passed, and thus check your progress so far. Follow it year by year, and you are guaranteed a life to remember...

PERSONAL DETAILS

This life planner is the property and responsibility of:

Name:..

Date of birth:..

Successive addresses throughout life   Successive phone numbers

1..   ....

2..   ....

3..   ....

4..   ....

5..   ....

6..   ....

7..   ....

8..   ....

9..   ....

10..   ....

Family background

Mother:..

Father:...

Brothers:...

....

....

Sisters:...

....

....

Sons:...

....

....

Daughters:..

....

....

Other relatives of note:...

....

....

INSTRUCTIONS FOR USE

1) CONSULT THE INSTRUCTIONS FOR EACH YEAR OF YOUR LIFE AS YOU REACH IT.

This is best done on your birthday, so make it an annual habit. Record your progress where indicated, and tick off each completed year in the index.

2) IF YOU ARE A NEWBORN, YOU SHOULD OBVIOUSLY START FROM YEAR 0.

You are allowed to ask a parent, sibling or friend to assist you in using this book until you are old enough to read and write.

3) IF YOU HAVE ALREADY STARTED YOUR LIFE, FOLLOW THIS BOOK FROM YOUR CURRENT AGE.

But also make sure to go through all the previous years to check that you have fulfilled essential stages. If you are 53 and still a virgin for instance, you must catch up asap by following the instructions for Age 17.

4) YOU MUST FOLLOW EACH YEAR'S INSTRUCTIONS TO THE LETTER.

They are based on cultural dictates, from which you stray at the risk of ostracism and personal ridicule from other, better-adjusted members of Western society. There are, however, legitimate exceptions: gays and lesbians should make obvious adjustments for years 11, 14, 17, 20, 30, 33, 36, 43, 46, 57, 71, 76 and 92. And women may want to allocate more time for motherhood, in which case they can skip years 32, 34, 35, 38 and 59.

5) IN THIS DAY AND AGE, YOU SHOULD AIM TO LIVE UNTIL 100.

If, however, you plan to depart earlier, simply bring forward essential life stages 86, 87, 97 and 100.

LIFE INDEX

Tick each year as you complete it,
to confirm you are ready to progress to the next.
By the end of your life, all these boxes must be ticked!

0	Make your birth unforgettable	■	24	Waste this year	■
1	Learn to babble incoherently	■	25	Have a quarterlife crisis	■
2	Master your bodily functions	■	26	Start working for the man	■
3	Become sexually attracted		27	Meet the love of your life	■
	to your Mommy or Daddy	■	28	Get hitched	■
4	Attempt to murder your		29	Get a mortgage	■
	younger siblings	■	30	Procreate	■
5	Make your first friends	■	31	Make a doomed attempt	
6	Make your first enemies	■		to stay in shape	■
7	Ask adults stupid questions	■	32	Turn into a workaholic	■
8	Let TV start controlling		33	Live the nuclear	
	your mind	■		family dream	■
9	Pester your parents for		34	Write the novel that is in you	■
	unaffordable consumer goods	■	35	Scratch your seven-year itch	■
10	Decide what you want		36	Burden your kids with	
	to be when you grow up	■		unreasonable expectations	■
11	Develop a crush on		37	Have an early midlife crisis	■
	your teacher	■	38	Climb the career ladder	■
12	Wrestle with your hormones	■	39	Deny your age	■
13	Go from loving to		40	Grow up	■
	hating your parents	■	41	Begin therapy	■
14	Investigate the other sex	■	42	Move to the suburbs	■
15	Rebel against society	■	43	Join the swinging scene	■
16	Start a band	■	44	Enjoy the finer things in life	■
17	Lose your virginity	■	45	Adopt a third world orphan	■
18	Officially become an adult	■	46	Divorce messily	■
19	Find yourself	■	47	Abandon the	
20	Sleep around	■		American Dream	■
21	Drink legally	■	48	Fight the flab	■
22	Acquire a higher education	■	49	Be abducted by aliens	■
23	Conquer the world	■	50	Become right-wing	■

This book is based on wide consultations with medical, religious and media authorities. We have tried to remain faithful to the clichés of individualistic Western society. Where there was disagreement on what constituted appropriate behavior for any particular year, reference was made to magazine surveys and Hollywood screenplays of the last decade.

AGE 0: MAKE YOUR BIRTH UNFORGETTABLE

Some options:
- Come out laughing
- Come out with a full head of hair
- Come out fully dressed
- Come out fully grown
- Come out holding your mother's appendix
- Refuse to come out until your demands are met

A successful birth is important if you want to get off to a good start in life. What you are looking for is to create a memorable occasion, which will shock the most jaded midwife and make the front pages.

RECORD THE DETAILS OF YOUR BIRTH FOR POSTERITY

Time:.................................... Place:..............................
Doctor's signature:..
Details of delivery:..
....
....

Method: Natural ■ Caesarian ■ Standing up ■ Lying down ■
Location: In a bed ■ In a field ■ In an alley ■ In a car ■
Father's behavior: Calm and collected ■ Panicked ■ Drunk ■
Mother's behavior: Calm and collected ■ Panicked ■ Drunk ■
Did you cry at birth: Yes, like a baby ■ No ■
Social circumstances: Promising ■ Unpromising ■
Number of prospective parents present at birth: 1 ■ 2 ■ 3 ■ 4 ■
Social class: Upper ■ Upper middle ■ Lower middle ■ Lower working ■
Weight:.......................... Degree of pinkness: ■ ■ ■ ■ ■ ■ ■ ■ ■
First impression of your mother:...
First impression of your father:..

CHECKLIST

Toes (circle): 1 2 3 4 5 6 7 8 9 10
Fingers: 1 2 3 4 5 6 7 8 9 10
Genitalia (tick):   Male ■   Female ■
Stomach: ■   Liver: ■   Heart: ■
Kidneys: 1 ■ 2 ■
Nose: ■   Eyes: 1 ■ 2 ■   Ears: 1 ■ 2 ■
Hairs on head (number):......................................

Midwife's prediction:
Will be ugly ■
Will be beautiful ■
Will be rich ■

AGE 1: LEARN TO BABBLE INCOHERENTLY

① On the town

Tarkovsky's films force one to stare back through the camera at one's own inner eye, don't you think?

Babaratapa baraagoooooga blabablara...

Your first year will be busy, but make sure to set time aside for babbling. Besides keeping your parents guessing whether you are cute or in fact retarded, babbling incoherently will prove an essential skill throughout your whole life. Here are some examples of future occasions when it will come in useful.

AGE 2: MASTER YOUR BODILY FUNCTIONS

Most of your internal organs should
be up and running smoothly by now,
but the bladder and bowels still require
your attention. Study this diagram
and learn how to operate them.

BLADDER

No. 1a) When your bladder wall is stretched, your sensory neurons will
carry a signal to your cerebrum via the sacral segments of your spinal cord.
Be sure to pick up on this signal.

No. 1b) Once you have made your way to a suitable location (such as
potty, or toilet), prepare your cerebrum to send a series of signals back to
the relevant muscles via your parasympathetic fibers.

No. 1c) Order your urethral sphincter muscle to relax.

No. 1d) Decontract your pelvic floor muscles to allow unimpeded flow.

No. 1e) Contract your detrusor muscles to allow the urine into the urethra.

No. 1f) Urinate.

No. 1g) Once your urinary bladder is empty, reverse all the signals.

BOWELS

No. 2a) Wait for an hour approximately after the ingestion of food, as the
waste material is processed along your digestive tract.

No. 2b) Gather the fecal matter in your rectum ampulla.

No. 2c) Monitor your rectal wall stretch receptors for signs of fullness.

No. 2d) Proceed to a suitable location (refer to *No. 1b*).

No. 2e) Push your diaphragm down to exert pressure on your digestive tract.

No. 2f) Force the walls of your anal canal apart so as to allow peristaltic
waves to propel the waste matter past your interior and exterior sphincters.

No. 2g) Gaze up at your parents, causing them to say "Big doodoo? Good
baby!" or similar.

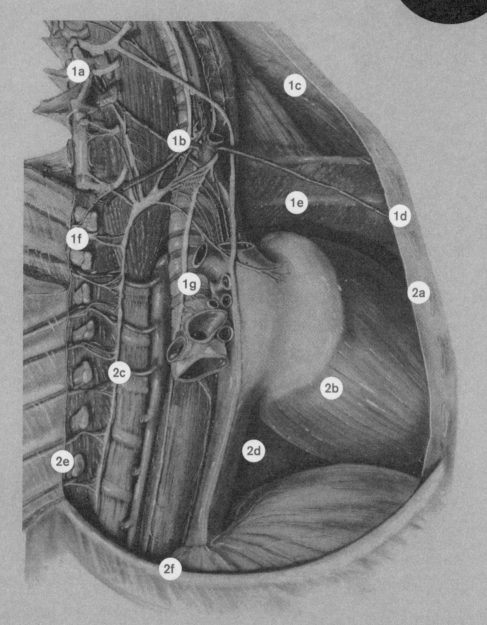

AGE 3: BECOME SEXUALLY ATTRACTED TO YOUR MOMMY OR DADDY

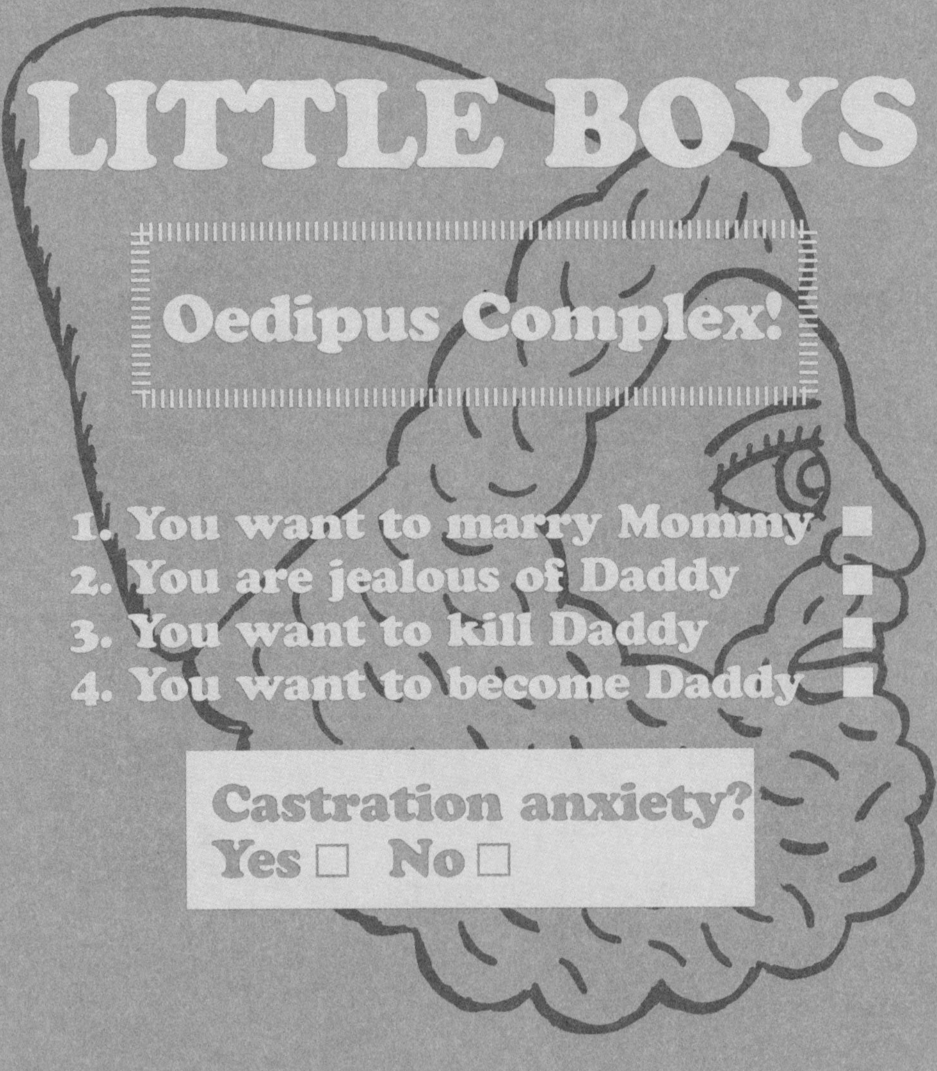

LITTLE BOYS

Oedipus Complex!

1. You want to marry Mommy ■
2. You are jealous of Daddy ■
3. You want to kill Daddy ■
4. You want to become Daddy ■

Castration anxiety?
Yes ☐   No ☐

As Sigmund Freud made clear, this is an unavoidable part of growing up. It is slightly embarrassing for all concerned, but you must get through it in order to become a balanced human being and enjoy a healthy sex life later on (cf ages 11, 14, 17, 20, 27, 28, 30, 35, 43, 76). Tick off each psychosexual stage as you reach it.

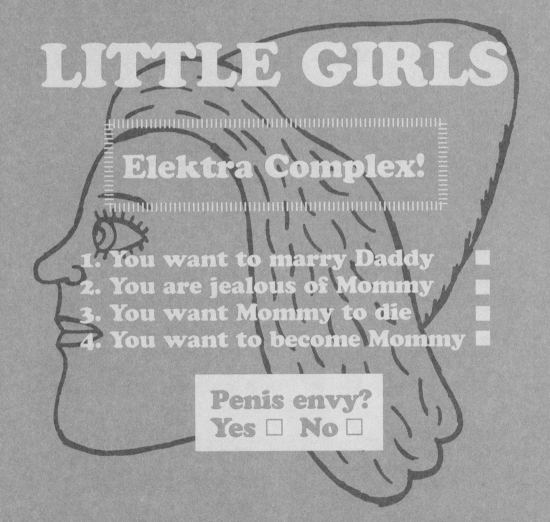

LITTLE GIRLS

Elektra Complex!

1. You want to marry Daddy ■
2. You are jealous of Mommy ■
3. You want Mommy to die ■
4. You want to become Mommy ■

Penis envy?
Yes ☐ No ☐

Well done! You may now relax until puberty (unless you did actually kill Mommy or Daddy).

AGE 4: ATTEMPT TO MURDER YOUR YOUNGER SIBLINGS

How to make it sound like an accident

"She was trying to fly!"

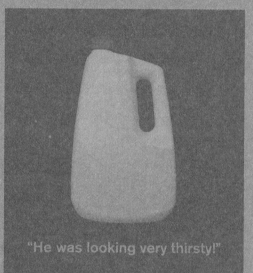

"He was looking very thirsty!"

"He wanted a swim!"

"We were playing doctors and nurses!"

Assassination attempts on your kid brother or sister are an inevitable rite of passage, both for you and for them. They are, after all, trying to usurp you. The minimum age for criminal responsibility is seven years old in most states, so you will probably not go to jail—although you may well be sent to your room for some considerable time.

"The washing machine ate her!"

"He bit Rex's tail!"

"She ate all Mommy's lollies!"

Examples of offenses that justify the murder of siblings:

•Playing with your toys
•Stroking your pet
•Making noises
•Eating your Lego
•Distracting Mommy
•Distracting Daddy
•Distracting Grandma
•Distracting Grandad
•Refusing to obey orders
•Usurping you

AGE 5: MAKE YOUR FIRST FRIENDS

My First Friends Checklist Candidate	 Big house	Latest games console	Swimming pool	Plasma screen TV
Jennifer (example)	✓	✓	✓	✓
Dwayne (example)	✗	✗	✗	✗

Now that you are at kindergarten, you are in a position to select your first proper friends. Remember: they will stay with you forever, probably even making awkward speeches about you at your wedding. Pick them carefully, with the help of this checklist.

Rich parents	Generous with pocket money	Well-stocked fridge	College trust fund	Pass?
✓	✓	✓	✓	Yes!
✗	✓	✗	✗	No

AGE 6: MAKE YOUR FIRST ENEMIES

EXAMPLE

TO ....Dwayne............'S DADDY:

Your son/~~daughter~~ has offended
me through the following behavior:

..........Called me a "dickwad"

My daddy will therefore
beat you up in revenge.

Time....After school

Place..Pizza Hut carpark

BE THERE OR ELSE!

TO ....'S DADDY:

Your son/daughter has offended
me through the following behavior:

My daddy will therefore
beat you up in revenge.

Time..................................

Place..................................

BE THERE OR ELSE!

TO ....'S DADDY:

Your son/daughter has offended
me through the following behavior:

My daddy will therefore
beat you up in revenge.

Time..................................

Place..................................

BE THERE OR ELSE!

TO ....'S DADDY:

Your son/daughter has offended
me through the following behavior:

My daddy will therefore
beat you up in revenge.

Time..................................

Place..................................

BE THERE OR ELSE!

As your socialization proceeds and you interact with your peer group, you will find that not all of them are to your taste. And some might not like you much either. Once you get past the initial shock, you must use the opportunity to make an "enemy." To ensure it's official, use the forms below.

TO ....'S DADDY:

Your son/daughter has offended me through the following behavior:
....
....
....

My daddy will therefore
beat you up in revenge.

Time..
Place...

BE THERE OR ELSE!

TO ....'S DADDY:

Your son/daughter has offended me through the following behavior:
....
....
....

My daddy will therefore
beat you up in revenge.

Time..
Place...

BE THERE OR ELSE!

TO ....'S DADDY:

Your son/daughter has offended me through the following behavior:
....
....
....

My daddy will therefore
beat you up in revenge.

Time..
Place...

BE THERE OR ELSE!

TO ....'S DADDY:

Your son/daughter has offended me through the following behavior:
....
....
....

My daddy will therefore
beat you up in revenge.

Time..
Place...

BE THERE OR ELSE!

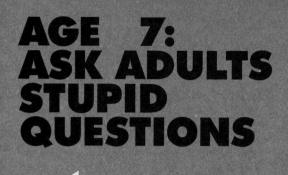

AGE 7:
ASK ADULTS
STUPID
QUESTIONS

INNOCENT QUESTIONS

Why do flowers smell so nice?

Does God have a Mommy and Daddy?

What makes the moon white?

Why can't I undo my belly button?

What do clouds taste like?

Where do flowers go when they die?

Grown-ups know all there is to know. Make the most of them by asking questions about everything that pops into your hyperactive little mind. Here are some common questions to get you started.

DIFFICULT QUESTIONS →

Why are people nasty?

Why can't flies fly with their wings sliced off?

What's a "virgin"?

Why are you wearing Mommy's panties?

Why does Grandpa smell?

What happens if my parents don't pay you the ransom?

AGE 8: LET TV START CONTROLLING YOUR MIND

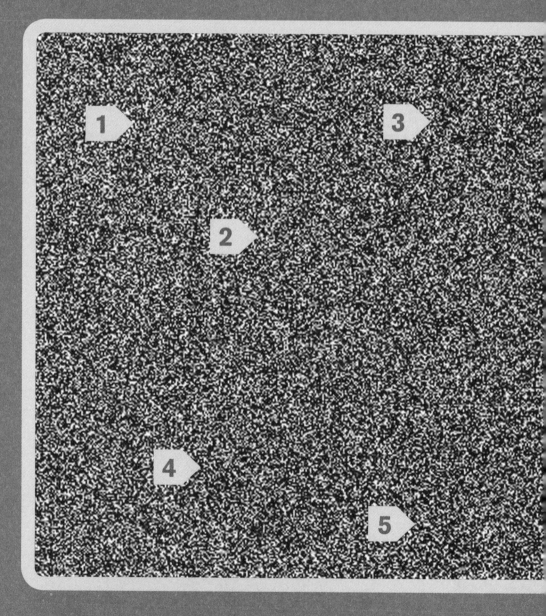

You will spend a considerable proportion of the next 92 years of your life watching television. Make sure you pick up on the subliminal instructions that are being beamed to you electronically. Study this TV screen, and learn to spot the subconscious messages contained therein.

1. "Don't use conditioner? Your hair will fall out for sure."
2. "Vote for Senator Gruber on Nov 9th!"
3. "Without a gold card, no one will love you, ever."
4. "The police are your very best friends and don't you forget it."
5. "Poor? It's your fault, you redneck loser."
6. "Multinational corporations mean you well, even though sometimes it may not seem like it."

AGE 9: PESTER YOUR PARENTS FOR UNAFFORDABLE CONSUMER GOODS

Parents surrender and buy you whatever you want

Parents's personality shatters

Parents contemplate self-harm

Parents contemplate infanticide

Parents try going to their "happy place"

Parents shout at you to shut up

I WANT IT! I WANT IT!

Start
here

At 9, it is time to face your responsibilities as a consumer, and use your newly developed pester power to make your mark on the global economy. The secret of pester power is relentless nagging—repeating your demands again and again until you have broken your parents down, reducing them to empty, dehumanized shells of their former selves. Here is a rough guide to what it takes.

I WANT IT! I WANT IT!

Parents ignore
you calmly

Parents ignore
you angrily

Parents
reason
with you

Parents
plead
with you

Parents
tell you to
be quiet

AGE 10: DECIDE WHAT YOU WANT TO BE WHEN YOU GROW UP

A Dream Jobs	Tick	B Steady Jobs	Tick
Astronaut		Doctor	
Firefighter		Stockbroker	
Secret agent		Principal	
Lifeguard		Investment banker	
Baseball player		Antiques dealer	
NBA player		Architect	
NFL player		Dentist	
Racing car driver		Professor	
Rock star		Judge	
Movie star		Mayor	
Supermodel		Chief executive	
Brain surgeon		Historian	
Rocket scientist		Advertising executive	
Ballerina		Journalist	
Bestselling author		Diplomat	
Pilot		Veterinarian	
TV anchor		Criminal lawyer	
President		Commercial lawyer	
Pirate		Family lawyer	
Ice cream tester		Divorce lawyer	

WELL DONE! Your first and most pleasant
decade is behind you. Now you must face reality
and look ahead to the serious business of living.
Here are the options. Pick from the column that
corresponds to your intellectual aptitude.

C Everyday Jobs	Tick	D Thankless Jobs	Tick
Waiter		Janitor	
Bookkeeper		Checkout person	
Bus driver		Burger flipper	
Computer programmer		Used car salesman	
Secretary		Repo man	
Hairdresser		Traffic warden	
Real estate agent		Garbage collector	
Insurance broker		Agony aunt	
IT consultant		Bodyguard	
Accountant		Hangman	
Middle manager		Tax lawyer	
Librarian		Tax collector	
Mechanic		Pizza delivery person	
Milkman		Dog walker	
Office worker		Prostitute	
Receptionist		Pimp	
Gardener		Porn film extra	
Teacher		Drug dealer	
Filing clerk		Artist	
Mailman		Undertaker	

AGE 11: DEVELOP A CRUSH ON YOUR TEACHER

Class: Biology

Ex. 23 Plant growth: Describe the main function of each of these flower parts.

HEAD: Spreads seeds

ROOTS: Supply the plant with water

LEAVES: Where photosynthesis happens

PETALS: Look beautiful, just like you, Miss

Class: Physics

Force field (44b)

ME → ME → ME → ME → ME → ME → ME → ME → ME → ME → ME → ME →

Electrons

You!

Class: French

Jacques mange un baguette. Il est un garcon. Son age est onze an. Jacques habite dans Paris. Paris es le capital de la France. Je t'aime! Je t'adore!! Pour toujour! Jacques avait une soeur Emilie, mais elle est dans Amerique pour visite le oncle de Jaques, qui est Ronald. Ronald habite a Washington D.C.

Eleven is the last age at which you will be able to enjoy an innocent infatuation, untainted by sexual tension. Make the most of it by going sweet on one of your sixth-grade teachers. Of course, it's no fun if they don't know about it. Here is how to encrypt your love right into your homework.

Class: Geography

Assignment due: Feb 10
Geology of local area

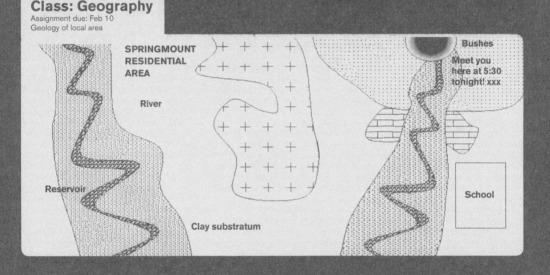

Class: Math

A motor oil manufacturer claims that their new oil saves 10% of the gasoline used by a normal car. If you drive 14,000 miles a year and you currently get 25 miles out of a gallon of gasoline, how many gallons of gasoline could you save in 1 year?

$$\frac{14,000 \text{ miles}}{25 \text{ miles per gallon}} = 560 \text{ gallons}$$

$$560 \text{ gallons} \times 0.10 = 56 \text{ gallons}.$$

P.S. I'm not sure this is right! Can we test it in your car this weekend Mr. Brooks? Puhleeeeeze.

Class: Art

AGE 12: WRESTLE WITH YOUR HORMONES

At 12, childhood is over. Now begins the furious battle that is puberty. But don't just sit there as your hormones turn your brain into a seething biological mush: actively reduce the levels of hormonal activity in your body, by exposing it to hormone-disrupting man-made chemicals as recommended below.

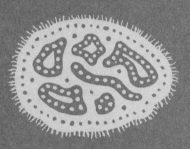

Natural hormone: *Testosterone*
Damage caused: Acne
Chemical defense: Rub DEHP-containing plastics onto your skin

Natural hormone: *Prolactin*
Damage caused: Mood swings
Chemical defense: Shower in fenarimol-rich pesticide

Natural hormone: *Dihydrotestosterone*
Damage caused: Involuntary erections
Chemical defense: Douse yourself with pyrethroids-based mosquito spray

Natural hormone: *Estrogen*
Damage caused: Menstruation
Chemical defense: Lick the PCBs out of a fluorescent lightbulb

Natural hormone: *Prostacyclin*
Damage caused: Wet dreams
Chemical defense:
Drink water contaminated with
Diethylstilbesterol DES

Natural hormone: *Progesterone*
Damage caused: Greasy hair
Chemical defense: Breathe in the
biphenyl-A off diesel fumes

Natural hormone: *Thyrotropin*
Damage caused: Smelly sweat
Chemical defense: Eat vegetables
treated with Trifluralin

Natural hormone: *Erythropoietin*
Damage caused: Awkward posture
Chemical defense: Swallow
DDE-packed insecticides

Natural hormone: *Androgen*
Damage caused: Pubic hair growth
Chemical defense:
Eat Polybrominated biphenyls-
contaminated food

Natural hormone: *Leutotrienes*
Damage caused: Voice breaking
Chemical defense: Eat fish
contaminated with Hexachlorobenzenes

AGE 13: GO FROM LOVING TO HATING YOUR PARENTS

BEFORE

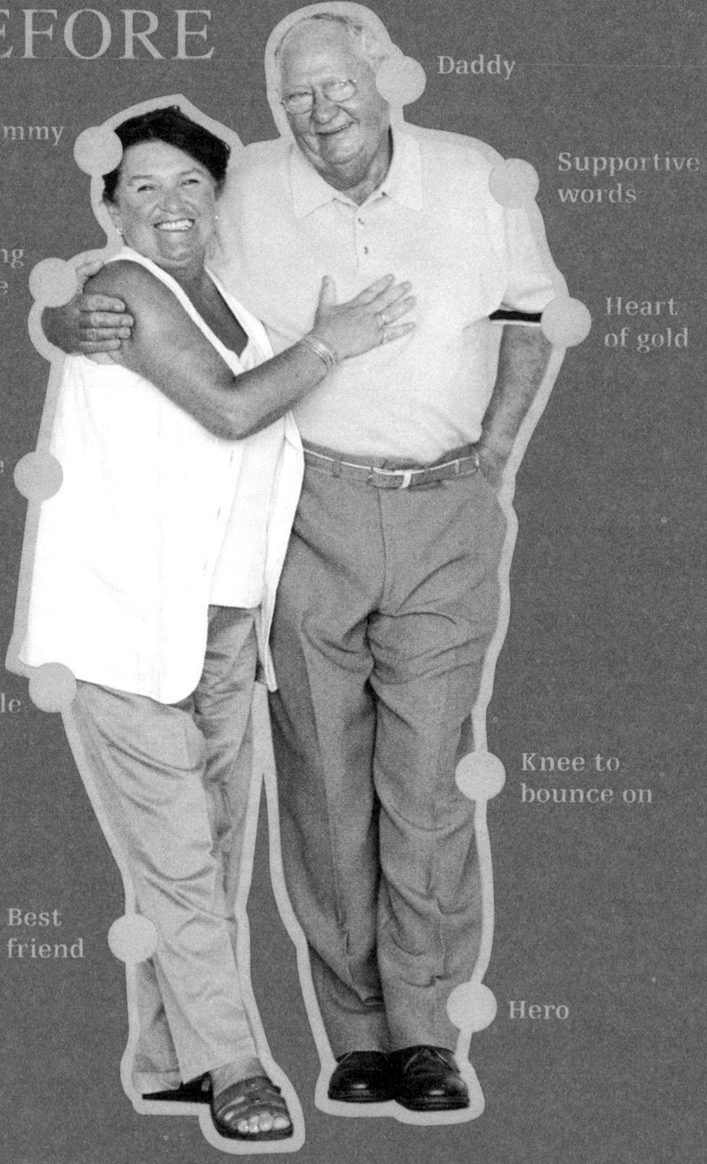

Daddy

Mommy

Supportive words

Loving smile

Heart of gold

Protective embrace

Huggable jumper

Knee to bounce on

Best friend

Hero

Month 1: Love

Many children worry they won't be able to achieve this radical transformation in feelings toward Mommy and Daddy. When they reach 13, though, most find it comes very naturally. Some achieve it overnight, others will need a little longer. Just relax and let nature take its course, monitoring the transition below.

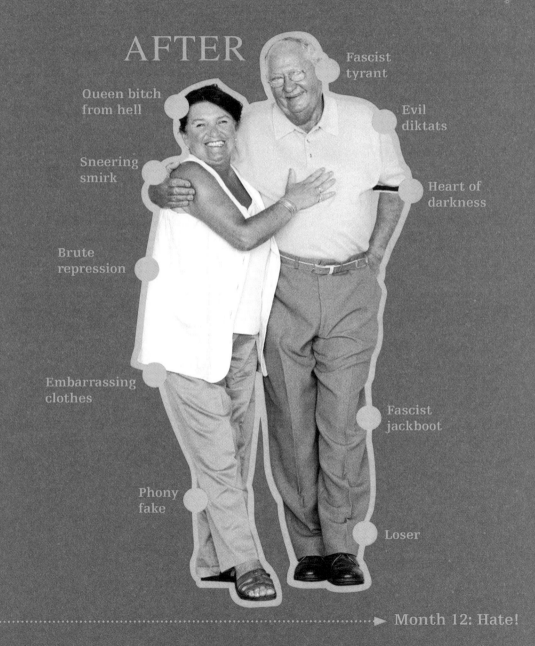

AFTER

Fascist tyrant

Queen bitch from hell

Evil diktats

Sneering smirk

Heart of darkness

Brute repression

Embarrassing clothes

Fascist jackboot

Phony fake

Loser

Month 12: Hate!

AGE 14: INVESTIGATE THE OTHER SEX

Haha yeah so today my best friend .... was talking to this really hot guy/girl .... in english class and they were basically talking about dating and stuff. Anyway, ... looked over my way and smiled and said something into ....'s ear and they both laughed. I'm not sure what it means. He/she is cute but I also have feelings for ....! I'm really confuzzed. I kinda avoided them after school and then I bumped into .... and ohmigod the CRAZIEST thing ever happened to him when he was on the way to the mall, he saw .... and .... like making out!!! I can't believe it, such a slut lol. Everyone knows .... was going with .... until .... got off with .... Seriously hilarious. Yeah anyway so then my friend .... came up and said you know what .... said before was that you were kinda hot! I could literally have DIED I blushed SOOO red. Anyway we then went back to class and I was like, I'm not looking at them, and they were like the same although I couldn't really see cuz they were sitting behind me, sometimes I think I have a gift.

Whatever. Did I mention that .... had told .... that I told............. about .... kissing ....? Anyway we were like, NO WAY! We laughed until we cried, it was the funniest thing ever! I guess you had to be there. So, I kinda have a thing for this other boy/girl .... but I'm not sure he/she feels the same way. There was that time in math when he/she looked at me and I thought he/she smiled but then I thought no way he/she is SOOOO out of my league, and then I said the stupidist thing I can't even say it here it's SO embarrassing but anyway it was too late. ARG! Oh well. I haven't spoken to .... in the longest time. I really really like him/her. A lot. But today, he/she called me and said that he/she really liked .... and then I called .... to tell him/her that .... had called me and he/she wanted to know if I had ....'s number but I told him/her that I didn't and that I would call .... to see if he/she did. He/she didn't. Why does it have to be so difficult? Sometimes I think my love is doomed. Life seriously sucks. *Sigh* Thank God for spring break!!!

AGE 15: REBEL AGAINST SOCIETY

Fifteen is the highlight of the teenage years, the age when you must expose the rest of the world to the full depth of your teenage anger and incomprehension. And make sure the world takes notice, or your rebellion will have been in vain. Ask the social authorities in your life to confirm you have indeed rebelled, by signing this diploma, which you may then hang in your teenage den.

Requirements:

❶ 15-year-old must have defied your authority repeatedly, engaged in shouting matches, door-slamming, prolonged sulking, made unsubstantiated allegations of general unfairness, claimed on at least five occasions that they had "not asked to be born."

❷ 15-year-old must have engaged in behavior that brought them to your attention and wasted valuable police time, such as graffitiing, underage drinking, congregating in shopping malls in a threatening manner, shoplifting.

❸ 15-year-old must have sat at the back of your class on a regular basis, disrupted lessons, handed homework in late, dressed in black, smoked tobacco on school premises, skipped at least six classes, and been sent to the principal's office at least twice.

❹ 15-year-old must have loitered around your premises in the company of other 15-year-olds, faked interest in some of your goods, then attempted to shoplift a minor item before feigning innocence once caught by security.

DIPLOMA

We hereby certify that

....

*has successfully rebelled against society
and is thereby free to proceed to sixteen.*

1 ....

MOTHER   FATHER

2 ....

LOCAL LAW ENFORCEMENT OFFICER

3 ....

TEACHER

4 ....

LOCAL RETAILER

AGE 16: START A BAND

RECTAL PROLAPSE

The Fuck Buddies

Apple Pie Overdose

GROTTEN SCROTUM

Every self-respecting teenager dreams of rock stardom. 16 is the right time to act upon that dream. Muster whatever friends and musical talent you possess, and give it your best shot. Here are some appropriately offensive band names to inspire you.

TOE JAM

ATOMIC TAMPAX

The Dead Grandads

P.T.A GANGBANG

EVISCERATOR 3000

SUBURBAN CRACK ATTACK

THE DOUCHE BAGS

COLUMBINE COMBO

AGE 17: LOSE YOUR VIRGINITY

Girls:

BOY NEXT DOOR ☐

PROS: sweet, no diseases, not far to travel
CONS: clumsy courtship, fumbling sex

OLDER MAN ☐

PROS: smooth, experienced, will pay for dinner
CONS: jealous wife, tearful kids

TALL, DARK STRANGER ☐

PROS: tall, dark
CONS: stranger

FAMILY MEMBER ☐

PROS: no "meet my parents" awkwardness
CONS: too many to list, avoid unless
brought up in a trailer

17 is the correct age to lose your virginity. 0 to 15 is illegal in most states. 16 is a bit keen. But 18 just doesn't have an erotic ring to it. The next issue is: who to lose your virginity to? Here are the options available; tick the one you have gone for.

Boys:

GIRL NEXT DOOR ☐

PROS: cute, no diseases, not far to travel
CONS: not particularly kinky

OLDER WOMAN ☐

PROS: experience, kudos
CONS: cliché

"PROFESSIONAL" ☐

PROS: guaranteed loss of virginity
CONS: potentially unhygienic,
costs pocket money

FAMILY PET ☐

PROS: might squeal but won't gossip
CONS: avoid unless brought up on a farm

AGE 18: OFFICIALLY BECOME AN ADULT

CLASSIC RITES OF PASSAGE

SEPIK (NEW GUINEA)
Strip naked, and let your elders carve hundreds of cuts into your skin over a period of hours so that you resemble a sacred crocodile. Heal, very slowly.

INUIT (ARCTIC)
Let yourself be strapped to poles planted in the snow in the arctic midwinter for a week, before being taken down and shot at, in order to attain "intimacy with death."

CONGRATULATIONS! At 18, you have come of age, and are finally ready to become a fully-fledged member of society. Mark the occasion with one of the classic rites of passage below. They all involve some degree of suffering, but this is essential if the world is to recognize the new, mature you.

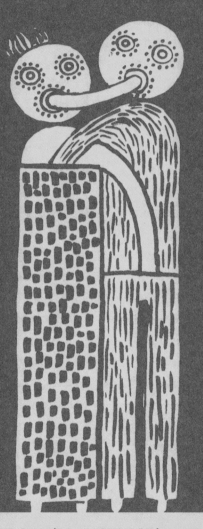

ARANDA (AUSTRALIA)

Allow yourself to be tossed in the air and hit with sticks, before being circumcised without anesthetic, and having your name carved on your forehead.

PROM (N. AMERICA)

Let your elders dress you in painful traditional clothing, then gyrate to terminal social ridicule whilst absorbing toxic substances which you will regurgitate as dawn breaks.*

*A common alternative: Dress in black and take out your school with an AK-47. Warning: May affect your availability to perform some of the tasks ahead in this book.

AGE 19: FIND YOURSELF

Adaptable ☐	Controlling ☐	Emotional ☐	Hesitant ☐
Adventurous ☐	Cooperative ☐	Energetic ☐	Honest ☐
Affectionate ☐	Cowardly ☐	Enthusiastic ☐	Hospitable ☐
Aggressive ☐	Crafty ☐	Extravagant ☐	Humble ☐
Ambitious ☐	Craven ☐	Extroverted ☐	Hypocritical ☐
Angry ☐	Critical ☐		Hysterical ☐
Antisocial ☐	Crude ☐	Faithful ☐	
Anxious ☐	Cruel ☐	Fanatical ☐	Imaginative ☐
Apathetic ☐	Cunning ☐	Flamboyant ☐	Impatient ☐
Apologetic ☐	Curious ☐	Flexible ☐	Impulsive ☐
Arrogant ☐	Cynical ☐	Flippant ☐	Inconsiderate ☐
Articulate ☐		Flirtatious ☐	Indecent ☐
Assertive ☐	Deceitful ☐	Focused ☐	Indecisive ☐
Audacious ☐	Destructive ☐	Forgiving ☐	Indifferent ☐
	Detached ☐	Frank ☐	Indiscreet ☐
Boastful ☐	Determined ☐	Friendly ☐	Indulgent ☐
Bossy ☐	Dignified ☐	Fussy ☐	Inhibited ☐
Brave ☐	Disciplined ☐		Inquisitive ☐
	Dishonest ☐	Generous ☐	Insecure ☐
Calculating ☐	Disorganized ☐	Gentle ☐	Insensitive ☐
Callous ☐	Distant ☐	Gracious ☐	Intelligent ☐
Careful ☐	Dogmatic ☐	Greedy ☐	Intolerant ☐
Cautious ☐	Domineering ☐	Gregarious ☐	Intransigent ☐
Cheerful ☐		Grumpy ☐	Introverted ☐
Compulsive ☐	Easy-going ☐		Intuitive ☐
Conceited ☐	Eccentric ☐	Hateful ☐	Inventive ☐
Confident ☐	Egocentric ☐	Haughty ☐	Irresponsible ☐
Considerate ☐	Egomaniac ☐	Helpful ☐	Irritable ☐

The true purpose of a college education is to give you plenty of free time to solve your identity crisis. No one really knows you, so you may start with a blank slate and define yourself from scratch. Here are the 200 essential psychological traits: pick the five or six that you want to base your lifelong personality on.

Jealous ☐	Observant ☐	Reclusive ☐	Submissive ☐
Judgmental ☐	Obsessive ☐	Reliable ☐	Supportive ☐
	Open-minded ☐	Religious ☐	Suspicious ☐
Kind ☐	Opportunistic ☐	Resentful ☐	
	Optimistic ☐	Reserved ☐	Tactful ☐
Lazy ☐	Organized ☐	Resilient ☐	Talkative ☐
Lethargic ☐		Respectful ☐	Tense ☐
Logical ☐	Paranoid ☐	Righteous ☐	Thoughtful ☐
Loving ☐	Passionate ☐	Romantic ☐	Timid ☐
	Passive ☐	Rude ☐	Tolerant ☐
Manipulative ☐	Patient ☐	Ruthless ☐	Tough ☐
Masochistic ☐	Perceptive ☐		Trustworthy ☐
Materialistic ☐	Persistent ☐	Sadistic ☐	
Mean ☐	Persuasive ☐	Sarcastic ☐	Unhelpful ☐
Merciful ☐	Pessimistic ☐	Scared ☐	
Meticulous ☐	Polite ☐	Selfish ☐	Vain ☐
Miserly ☐	Pompous ☐	Sensitive ☐	Vindictive ☐
Modest ☐	Pragmatic ☐	Sensual ☐	Virtuous ☐
Moody ☐	Pretentious ☐	Sentimental ☐	Vivacious ☐
	Promiscuous ☐	Serious ☐	Vulgar ☐
Naïve ☐	Proud ☐	Shallow ☐	Vulnerable ☐
Nasty ☐	Prudent ☐	Shy ☐	
Nervous ☐	Psychotic ☐	Simple ☐	Warm ☐
Neurotic ☐		Sincere ☐	Weird ☐
	Quiet ☐	Smart ☐	Wicked ☐
Obedient ☐		Smelly ☐	Worldly ☐
Obnoxious ☐	Rational ☐	Squeamish ☐	
Obsequious ☐	Rebellious ☐	Stern ☐	Zany ☐

AGE 20: SLEEP AROUND

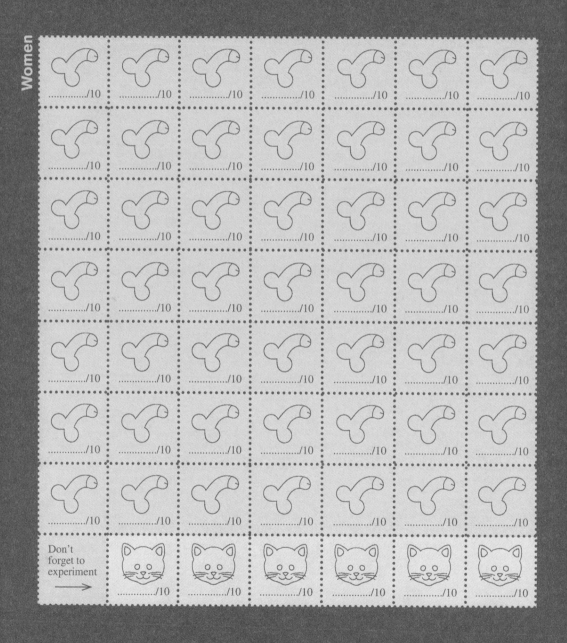

Women

............./10 ..../10 ..../10 ..../10 ..../10 ..../10 ..../10

............./10 ..../10 ..../10 ..../10 ..../10 ..../10 ..../10

............./10 ..../10 ..../10 ..../10 ..../10 ..../10 ..../10

............./10 ..../10 ..../10 ..../10 ..../10 ..../10 ..../10

............./10 ..../10 ..../10 ..../10 ..../10 ..../10 ..../10

............./10 ..../10 ..../10 ..../10 ..../10 ..../10 ..../10

Don't forget to experiment → ..../10 ..../10 ..../10 ..../10 ..../10

In a few years' time, you will be expected to enter a stable monogamous relationship with a view to forming a family unit. Your biological imperative this year, however, is to copulate with just about anyone, just about anywhere, just about anyhow. Rate mating partners below as you work your way through them. Keep the top-ranking partner's phone number: it may come in useful for age 27.

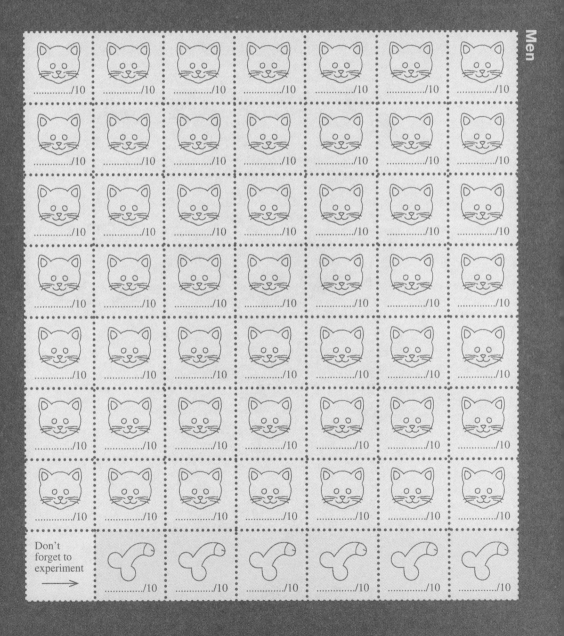

AGE 21: DRINK LEGALLY

At last, you are officially capable of coping with alcoholic beverages. And because you haven't had a drink for 21 years, you must make up for it. Make sure every liquid you absorb this year is alcoholic. Here are some recommended alcoholic substitutes for every drinking occasion.

Instead of coffee, drink:

Port
(intense, helps concentrate the mind)

Instead of water, drink:

Vodka
(same color, more interesting taste)

Instead of tea, drink:

Rum
(great for dunking cookies)

Instead of mouth freshener, drink:

Gin
(anti-bacterial properties
and fresh smell)

Instead of breastmilk, drink:

Champagne
(helps babies burp)

Instead of
sports drinks, drink:

Tequila
(full of sunny
Mexican energy)

Instead of milk, drink:

Crème de menthe
(same consistency and fat levels)

AGE 22: ACQUIRE A HIGHER EDUCATION

How much I have learned:

$..

Lecture: "Applied Genomics: Gene Identification"...............

Lecture: "Loneliness in the Works of Marcel Proust"...........

Lecture: "Computational Biophysics Imaging"...................

Lecture: "Mesopotamian Coinage: The Middle Period"..........

Lecture: "Post-feminist Agendas in Sylvia Plath's Poetry"......

Lecture: "Molecular Sequencing 101".........................

Lecture: "Advanced Modern French II"..........................

Lecture: "Advanced Modern Chinese II".........................

Lecture: "Patenting Nanotechnology: Legal Loopholes"..........

Lecture: "Representations of Bisexuality in 17th-Century Painting"....

Lecture: "Mathematical Models in Finance: Stochastic Equations".....

Lecture: "Intracranial Aneurysms in Neurological Surgery"..................

Lecture: "Drama: The Viking Oral Tradition"....................

Lecture: "Cell Biology: Eukaryotic Experimental Models".........

Lecture: "Hegel's Aesthetic Philosophy: A Revisionist Approach".......

Lecture: "Valuation: Dividend Discount Model vs. Multiples Model"....

Lecture: "Screenwriting for Beginners".........................

Lecture: "Namespaces in XML 1.1, SVG 1.1, and XSL (XSL-FO) 1.0".

Lecture: "Media Studies: Bypassing the Corporate Channels".........

While you are still in college, you might as well pick up an education, and if possible a degree. In today's high-tech global economy, a higher education is a prerequisite for success. Indeed, figures show that a college graduate will earn nearly $1 million more than a high school graduate over their lifetime. Here is how the figures break down course by course. Try to attend mostly lectures that teach you the lucrative kind of knowledge.

Value over a lifetime: $23,000

Value over a lifetime: $45

Value over a lifetime: $15,000

Value over a lifetime: $24.50

Value over a lifetime: $9

Value over a lifetime: $49,000

Value over a lifetime: $2,000

Value over a lifetime: $22,000

Value over a lifetime: $78,200

Value over a lifetime: $116

Value over a lifetime: $68,000

Value over a lifetime: $57,900

Value over a lifetime: $11

Value over a lifetime: $59,500

Value over a lifetime: $0.10

Value over a lifetime: $101,998

Value over a lifetime: $0–$1,000,000

Value over a lifetime: $62,109

Value over a lifetime: -$8,400

AGE 23: CONQUER THE WORLD

①

EIFFEL TOWER
(Paris, France)

Angle: Tradition dictates that this photo be taken from the Trocadero.

②

BIG BEN
(London, United Kingdom)

Angle: It is customary to use the zoom.

③

LEANING TOWER OF PISA
(Pisa, Italy)

Angle: Make sure you capture this exact incline from across the piazza.

④

BEER HALL
(Munich, Germany)

Angle: A simple shot, but must feature at least six beers.

At 23, the world is your oyster! You must range far and wide, so that you may bore everyone with your travel tales as you age. Take the following photos, and stick them on these pages as you travel. They will prove that you have indeed seen the world.

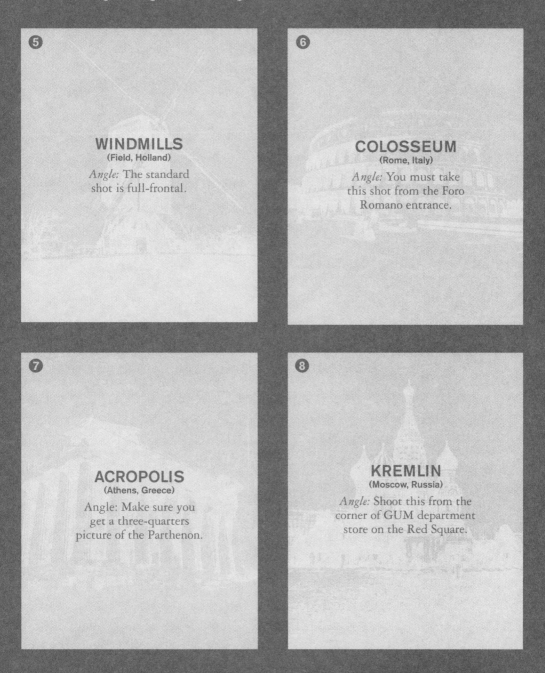

⑤

WINDMILLS
(Field, Holland)

Angle: The standard shot is full-frontal.

⑥

COLOSSEUM
(Rome, Italy)

Angle: You must take this shot from the Foro Romano entrance.

⑦

ACROPOLIS
(Athens, Greece)

Angle: Make sure you get a three-quarters picture of the Parthenon.

⑧

KREMLIN
(Moscow, Russia)

Angle: Shoot this from the corner of GUM department store on the Red Square.

AGE 24: WASTE THIS YEAR

Day 1: Sharpen your pencils
Day 2: Tidy your room
Day 3: Play air guitar
Day 4: Paint a self-portrait
Day 5: Listen to the wind
Day 6: Pick some flowers
Day 7: Replace your shoelaces
Day 8: Replace dead lightbulbs
Day 9: Sweep the chimney
Day 10: Weed the garden
Day 11: Mow the lawn
Day 12: Spy on your neighbors
Day 13: Look out the window
Day 14: Squeeze your pimples
Day 15: Moisturize the back of your knees
Day 16: Water your plants
Day 17: Stroke stray cats
Day 18: Make your own jam
Day 19: Bake your own bread
Day 20: Air your mattress
Day 21: Reread your favorite book
Day 22: Sweep the floor
Day 23: Tidy the attic
Day 24: Iron your tea towels
Day 25: Restart your computer
Day 26: Pick your nose
Day 27: Practice your headstanding technique
Day 28: Clean your ears
Day 29: Reorganize your fridge
Day 30: Shuffle paper into piles
Day 31: Scratch your itches
Day 32: Plan your outfits a week in advance
Day 33: Plan your hypothetical wedding
Day 34: Revise your signature
Day 35: Write a dirty limerick
Day 36: Yawn
Day 37: Go to the toilet
Day 38: File your nails
Day 39: Floss your teeth
Day 40: Channel surf
Day 41: Test if your breath smells
Day 42: Check your phone for missed calls
Day 43: Crack your knuckles
Day 44: Surf the net
Day 45: Iron your underwear
Day 46: Watch daytime TV
Day 47: Play Solitaire
Day 48: Roll your thumbs
Day 49: Wash your hair
Day 50: Rearrange your furniture
Day 51: Clean the oven
Day 52: Check your email
Day 53: Update your address book
Day 54: Daydream
Day 55: Think of a plot for a novel
Day 56: Turn a cardboard box into a racing car
Day 57: Copy out the lyrics to your favorite songs
Day 58: Call someone you haven't spoken to in ages
Day 59: Take a long hot shower
Day 60: Take a long hot bath
Day 61: Play dress-up

Day 62: Play video games
Day 63: Watch the shopping channels
Day 64: Write a list of names to call your children
Day 65: Make a castle out of matchsticks
Day 66: Pick a new screensaver for your computer
Day 67: Browse Friends Reunited
Day 68: Memorize useless facts
Day 69: Melt something
Day 70: Ring up your grandparents
Day 71: Go for a jog
Day 72: Snack between meals
Day 73: Buy your Christmas presents in advance
Day 74: Peel off a beer bottle label
Day 75: Watch the world go by
Day 76: Have a smoke
Day 77: Declutter your bag
Day 78: Make up a new insult
Day 79: Doodle
Day 80: Vacuum under your bed
Day 81: Make someone a cup of tea
Day 82: Debate politics with a stranger
Day 83: Babysit yourself
Day 84: Play make-believe
Day 85: Delete old numbers from your cellphone
Day 86: File your tax return
Day 87: Clean your computer with a cotton swab
Day 88: Stare at a magic eye poster
Day 89: Style your hair
Day 90: Chat on Internet chat rooms
Day 91: Make a mix tape
Day 92: Fly paper airplanes
Day 93: Play with yourself
Day 94: Pretend you're a Charlie's Angel
Day 95: Teach a toddler to swear
Day 96: Learn the alphabet backwards
Day 97: See how many grapes fit in your mouth
Day 98: Create the ultimate sandwich
Day 99: Talk to the mailman
Day 100: Talk to the milkman
Day 101: Talk to the newspaper boy
Day 102: Talk to the Jehovah's witness
Day 103: List all your heroes
Day 104: Change your ringtone
Day 105: Write your will
Day 106: List all your possessions
Day 107: Pin up a photo of your favorite celebrity
Day 108: Apply to go on Jerry Springer
Day 109: Leaf through holiday brochures
Day 110: Sew the buttons back onto your garments
Day 111: Wash the dishes
Day 112: Clean the windows
Day 113: Try to remember your childhood
Day 114: Count all of your friends
Day 115: Roll down a hill
Day 116: Measure your penis / bust
Day 117: Decide on your favorite color
Day 118: Clean your fingernails
Day 119: Design a new board game
Day 120: Try on all your clothes and see what still fits
Day 121: Throw away pens that don't work
Day 122: Make your own music

Day 123: Watch cartoons
Day 124: Paint your nails
Day 125: Do some coloring-in
Day 126: Give yourself a pedicure
Day 127: Create a new dance craze
Day 128: Pluck your eyebrows
Day 129: Shave your armpits
Day 130: Study a map
Day 131: Rearrange your desk
Day 132: Clip your toenails
Day 133: Make prank phone calls
Day 134: Look for lost socks
Day 135: Build an ant farm
Day 136: Write a review of a film
Day 137: Write a short story
Day 138: Write to Santa
Day 139: Hold your breath
Day 140: Play catch
Day 141: Update your iPod
Day 142: Flip through a women's magazine
Day 143: Eavesdrop on people's conversations
Day 144: Make a house of cards
Day 145: Do your spring cleaning
Day 146: Make up a joke
Day 147: Go out for ice cream
Day 148: Make a fish finger sandwich
Day 149: Read your junk mail
Day 150: Make your bed
Day 151: Fill in a questionnaire
Day 152: Call a call center
Day 153: Hand-wash all your clothes
Day 154: Vacuum the car
Day 155: Clean the garage
Day 156: Weigh yourself
Day 157: Color-coordinate your CD collection
Day 158: Alphabetize your spice rack
Day 159: Count your body hairs
Day 160: Christen your freckles
Day 161: Write a list of all your lists
Day 162: Try not to think about penguins
Day 163: Google yourself
Day 164: Google your parents
Day 165: Google your exes
Day 166: Google your friends
Day 167: Google your enemies
Day 168: Shred your receipts
Day 169: Stare at the back of people's heads
Day 170: Collect lint
Day 171: Make a rubber-band ball
Day 172: Take up trainspotting
Day 173: Take up planespotting
Day 174: Take up toupeespotting
Day 175: Learn origami
Day 176: Open and close your eyes very fast
Day 177: Repeat a word until it sounds strange
Day 178: Pluck your eyebrows
Day 179: Pluck your pubic hair
Day 180: Pluck your nostrils
Day 181: Feed the pigeons
Day 182: Hunt a cockroach
Day 183: Train your pet to play dead

At 24, you are on the cusp of real life, about to embark on the long struggle of career, family and self-reliance. This year is therefore intended for bumming around, getting up late, and wandering around in your bathrobe all day, usually at your parents' house. Here is how to procrastinate your way through the whole year, day by day.

Day 184: Practice yoga
Day 185: Imagine what you would rather be doing
Day 186: Invert your eyelids
Day 187: Practice your party trick
Day 188: List all the people you've kissed
Day 189: Read the dictionary
Day 190: Stare into space
Day 191: Pay your bills
Day 192: Look up when people walk past
Day 193: Look out the window
Day 194: Try and remember last week's dreams
Day 195: Tap your fingers on your desk
Day 196: Label all your underwear
Day 197: Design your ideal tattoo
Day 198: List what you would buy if you won the lotto
Day 199: Call your Mom
Day 200: Recall all the bad things you've ever done
Day 201: Bite your nails
Day 202: Create your own knock-knock joke
Day 203: Play tic-tac-toe
Day 204: Read your tarot cards
Day 205: Learn to play Su Do Ku
Day 206: Practice your bubble-gum blowing
Day 207: Peel grapes
Day 208: Play with your duvet
Day 209: Count to infinity
Day 210: Search the phone book for funny names
Day 211: Invest in a Rubik's cube
Day 212: Call customer service hotlines
Day 213: See how far you can lean back in your chair
Day 214: Try moving an inanimate object by "the force"
Day 215: Count your teeth using your tongue
Day 216: Plan your life from 0 to 100
Day 217: Scratch your head
Day 218: Send out "funny" email attachments
Day 219: Search for long-lost relatives online
Day 220: Count your paper-clip supplies
Day 221: Stalk a spider
Day 222: Count every second
Day 223: Read other people's horoscopes
Day 224: Whistle a whole symphony
Day 225: Proofread a famous novel
Day 226: Photograph all your possessions
Day 227: Stand in line for the sake of it
Day 228: Fill then empty your shopping trolley
Day 229: Memorize this list
Day 230: Write to the President
Day 231: Call wrong numbers
Day 232: Pray to another religion's gods
Day 233: Invent a swear word
Day 234: List your acquaintances
Day 235: Visualize everyone you meet naked
Day 236: Defluff your belly button
Day 237: Count the cracks in the ceiling
Day 238: Talk to yourself
Day 239: Read the fire extinguisher instructions
Day 240: Monitor your bowel movements
Day 241: Feed the cat
Day 242: Feed the pigeons
Day 243: Feed the ducks
Day 244: Feed the boa constrictor

Day 245: Check your country is in the atlas
Day 246: Watch the news
Day 247: Follow the stock market live
Day 248: Order a pizza of your own invention
Day 249: Ensure your golf balls are the right size
Day 250: Set a mousetrap
Day 251: Get drunk
Day 252: Clean your CDs
Day 253: Sort out your photo album
Day 254: Make mayonnaise
Day 255: Visit thiswebsitewillchangeyourlife.com
Day 256: Climb a tree
Day 257: Rate your exes
Day 258: Teach your parrot to swear
Day 259: Stay in bed
Day 260: Monitor the accuracy of weather reports
Day 261: Write an ugly poem
Day 262: Sort out your sock drawer
Day 263: Watch your hair grow
Day 264: Gaze at your navel
Day 265: Guesstimate the velocity of clouds
Day 266: Pimp your ride
Day 267: Learn to program the VCR
Day 268: Check all your food's sell-by dates
Day 269: Brush your teeth until they gleam
Day 270: Throw some dice
Day 271: Do drugs
Day 272: Calibrate your hourglass
Day 273: Change your pillowcase
Day 274: Replenish your stock of bookmarks
Day 275: Research your family tree
Day 276: Walk around the block
Day 277: Study the back of cereal packs
Day 278: Collect stamps today only
Day 279: Chew every mouthful ten times
Day 280: Start a blog
Day 281: Play chess against yourself
Day 282: Write until your pen runs out of ink
Day 283: Learn Pi
Day 284: Arrange flowers
Day 285: Iron your T-shirts
Day 286: Take your pulse
Day 287: Archive your emails
Day 288: Report cracks in the pavement
Day 289: Return a recent purchase
Day 290: Catch a fly then let it go
Day 291: Call friends whose name begins in "A"
Day 292: Rerecord your answerphone greeting
Day 293: Search your garden for snakes
Day 294: Keep an eye out for UFOs
Day 295: Search the papers for subliminal messages
Day 296: Defrost your freezer
Day 297: Descale your kettle
Day 298: Defragment your hard drive
Day 299: Burn toast
Day 300: Go to the gym
Day 301: Run errands
Day 302: Smell the coffee
Day 303: Ask God a direct question
Day 304: Do the crossword
Day 305: Record radio advertising for posterity

Day 306: Learn Morse code
Day 307: Comb your carpet
Day 308: Sleep in
Day 309: Sleep over
Day 310: Stalk a column of ants
Day 311: Listen to shopping mall music
Day 312: Wait for a payphone to ring
Day 313: Memorize today's stock market prices
Day 314: Read a book in a language you don't know
Day 315: Count the number of days since your birth
Day 316: Play "I spy"
Day 317: Flirt with someone telepathically
Day 318: Check your backyard for WMD
Day 319: Taste-test rival soft drinks
Day 320: Stockpile sugarcubes
Day 321: Check you're not on the FBI's wanted list
Day 322: Boast of things you've done in a dream
Day 323: Prune your geraniums
Day 324: Fight the power
Day 325: Read half a whodunnit
Day 326: Pinch yourself
Day 327: Erect your nipples
Day 328: Make yourself cry
Day 329: Clip some coupons
Day 330: Shave your legs
Day 331: Rake the leaves
Day 332: House-sit your own house
Day 333: Catch raindrops with your tongue
Day 334: Overegg a pudding
Day 335: Reread old love letters
Day 336: Window-shop
Day 337: Take out the garbage
Day 338: Sweep for cobwebs
Day 339: Tenderize meat
Day 340: Wish upon a star
Day 341: Experiment with different perfumes
Day 342: Make popcorn
Day 343: Loiter
Day 344: Swear in a foreign language
Day 345: Bark at passing dogs
Day 346: Make up new names for the stars
Day 347: Outstare yourself in the mirror
Day 348: Replant a flower
Day 349: Try and get two different species to mate
Day 350: Pick your favorite crater on the moon
Day 351: Find mistakes in your cookbooks
Day 352: Sell lemonade on the street corner
Day 353: Make plans for world domination
Day 354: Dissect a chicken nugget
Day 355: Call the talking clock
Day 356: Comb your eyebrows
Day 357: Revise your favorite color
Day 358: Work out your lucky number
Day 359: Walk the dog
Day 360: Walk the cat
Day 361: Monitor your calorie intake
Day 362: Plump your cushions
Day 363: Write to a long-lost relative
Day 364: Shine your shoes
Day 365: Hang out with a load of other 24-year-olds
NOW GET A LIFE!

AGE 25: HAVE A QUARTERLIFE CRISIS

Alexander the Great
(356 B.C.–323 B.C.)

By 25, had conquered most of Asia Minor and founded Alexandria.

Continents you have conquered:

....

....

....

....

....

Mozart
(1756–1791)

By 25, had performed in most major European courts and composed seven operas.

Major musical works you have composed:

....

....

....

....

Einstein allegedly observed that by the age of 25, you are all that you are ever going to be. And indeed, at 25, you are a quarter of your way through life. What exactly have you achieved? Compare your track record with that of other notable 25-year-olds and assess your progress.

Bill Gates
(1955–)

By 25, had founded Microsoft.

Billion-dollar world-leading companies you have founded:

....
....
....
....

Joan of Arc
(1412–1431)

By 25, had helped save France from the English, received direct divine guidance, and been burned at the stake.

Countries in which you are a national hero:

....
....
....
....

AGE 26:
START WORKING
FOR THE MAN

Standard Contract

I, ...,

hereby agree to spend the next 40 years of my life
working at least 8 hours a day (excluding weekends and
the odd vacation), for one or several corporations,
who may or may not fire me, as and when they see fit.

In return, I will receive some money to pay the bills
every month, a modest pension to survive on in old age,
and the satisfaction of knowing I have done my bit to boost
the aforesaid corporations' share price and dividends.

Signed and dated:

....

THE EMPLOYEE

....

THE MAN

At 26, your carefree youth is now largely behind you. It is time to enter the real world, which means getting a proper job. Jobs come in various shapes and sizes, but 99% of them have this in common: you will be working to make someone else money. Start getting used to it by signing this contract.

"The man"

AGE 27: MEET THE LOVE OF YOUR LIFE

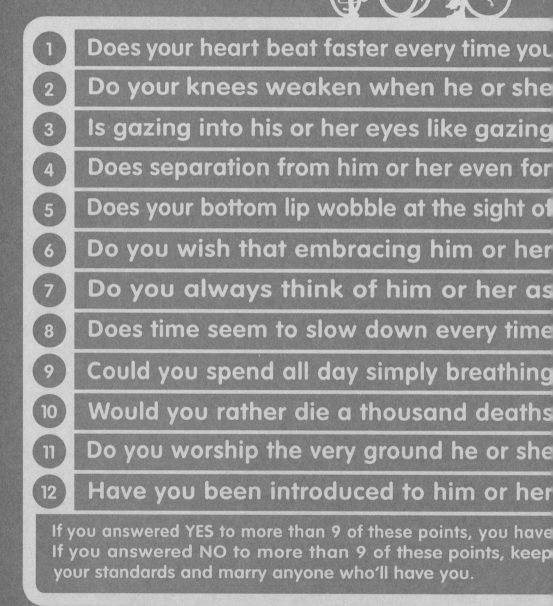

1. Does your heart beat faster every time you
2. Do your knees weaken when he or she
3. Is gazing into his or her eyes like gazing
4. Does separation from him or her even for
5. Does your bottom lip wobble at the sight of
6. Do you wish that embracing him or her
7. Do you always think of him or her as
8. Does time seem to slow down every time
9. Could you spend all day simply breathing
10. Would you rather die a thousand deaths
11. Do you worship the very ground he or she
12. Have you been introduced to him or her

If you answered YES to more than 9 of these points, you have
If you answered NO to more than 9 of these points, keep
your standards and marry anyone who'll have you.

By now, you should have sown most of your wild oats, and will be looking to secure a long-term partner, and preferably the love of your life. Here is a test you may use to assess potential candidates. We cannot guarantee that you will find "the one," of course, but this should help narrow down the field.

	Yes (tick)	No (tick)
see him or her?		
touches you?		
into infinity itself?		
an instant feel like torture?		
him or her talking to someone else?		
would never end?		
alone, quite alone?		
you look at him or her?		
in the smell of his or her skin?		
than live without him or her?		
she walks on?		
yet?		

met the love of your life. Congratulations! Now, get hitched. looking, at least until the age of 37, when you may compromise

AGE 28: GET HITCHED

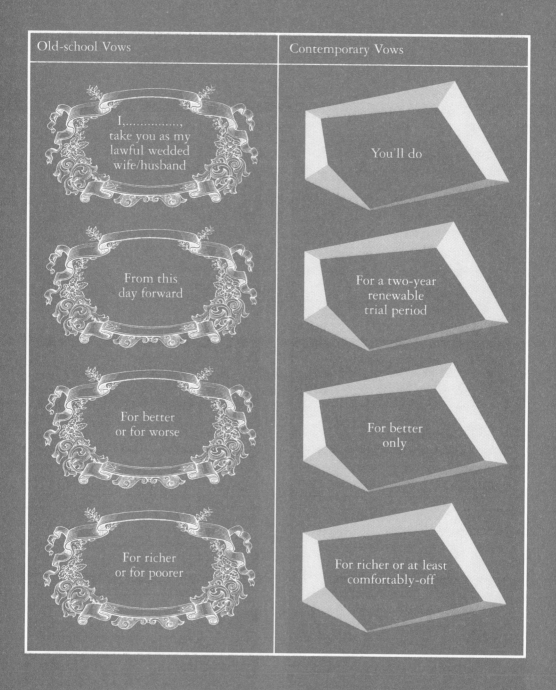

Old-school Vows	Contemporary Vows
I,..............., take you as my lawful wedded wife/husband	You'll do
From this day forward	For a two-year renewable trial period
For better or for worse	For better only
For richer or for poorer	For richer or at least comfortably-off

28 is an entirely suitable age to marry. The institution of marriage has changed much over the years, and, sadly, traditional wedding vows do not reflect today's realities. Customize your own, according to your tastes and preferences. Here is an alternative version that you are free to use. *Note: do warn the priest beforehand.*

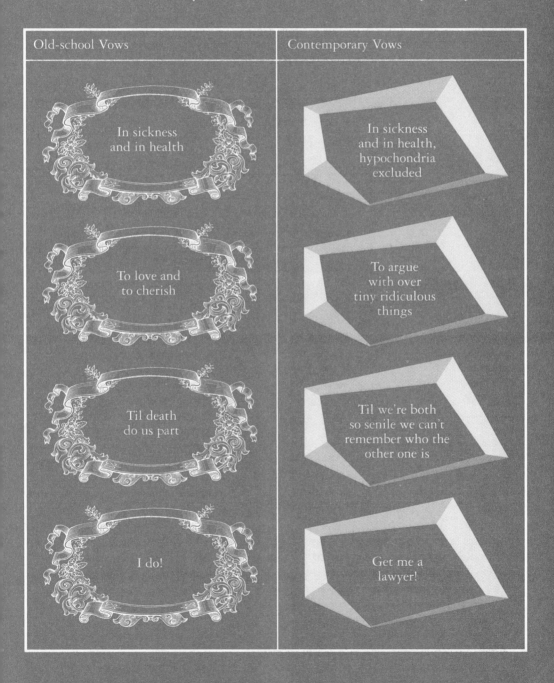

Old-school Vows	Contemporary Vows
In sickness and in health	In sickness and in health, hypochondria excluded
To love and to cherish	To argue with over tiny ridiculous things
Til death do us part	Til we're both so senile we can't remember who the other one is
I do!	Get me a lawyer!

AGE 29: GET A MORTGAGE

ROUGH SALARY: $2,000,000
*Dream of a huge mansion
with private beach and helipad!*

ROUGH SALARY: $1,000,000
*Dream of a duplex
on Fifth Avenue!*

ROUGH SALARY: $300,000
*Dream of a
midtown condo!*

ROUGH SALARY: $120,000
*Dream of a nice
house with a garden!*

Now that you're happily married, the next step is to buy your dream house. This is often portrayed as a complicated decision, full of legal pitfalls and financial headaches. In reality, however, only one thing matters: tailoring your dream to your means.

<u>ROUGH SALARY: $50,000</u>
Dream of a small apartment
in the middle of nowhere!

<u>ROUGH SALARY: $20,000</u>
Dream of a
crack-infested project!

<u>ROUGH SALARY: $10,000</u>
Dream of a trailer
in Tornado Alley!

<u>ROUGH SALARY: $0–$5,000</u>
Dream of a nice
warm cardboard box!

AGE 30: PROCREATE

After 30 years of carefree existence, it's time to face up to your primary purpose on this planet: the reproduction of the species. Here is a seven-point plan for conceiving as perfect a child as your genes will allow.

1. Pick a winner

Conception is a delicate and difficult process. Obviously, menstrual cycles, diet, and natural fertility all play a part. But the key factor is motivation. Both of you should visualize in your mind the particular spermatozoid you wish to see succeed, and cheer it along on its journey up the fallopian tubes.

2. Choose your moment

Plan your child's birthdate with care. Children born over the summer vacation or Christmas grow up without proper birthday parties, thus permanently damaging their self-esteem. The best days to conceive are January 8, July 21, and September 17. Worst day is February 26.

3. Hedge your bets

If you're experiencing difficulties getting pregnant, make sure you've explored all the options. Don't neglect age-old methods, such as medieval witchcraft: swallowing a couple of toad placentas marinated in bat sperm may just do the trick.

4. Work the womb

Don't let your child stew in the amniotic juice, bored and bone idle for nine months. Three hours of Latin audiotapes played against the belly button every day will stand it in good stead when it emerges onto the job market.

5. Deliver the goods

It is simply never too early to cultivate a sense of initiative in your child. What better challenge than to let them find their own way out of the womb? Ask the midwife to stand back and give your precious offspring the chance to enter the world unaided. N.B. You may help them cut the umbilical cord.

6. Shape your child's future

As everyone knows, the infant's head is still relatively soft at birth. Take a few minutes to knead it into the most becoming shape—your child will thank you later. Hint: prominent cheekbones are attractive in both sexes.

7. Name to shame

Kids with ridiculous names learn to try harder in life. Stiffen your child's moral fiber with a name that will get him or her victimized on the playground. Call an ugly girl "Princess," for instance, or a sickly boy "Rambo."

Repeat steps 1 to 7 for every child. Current limits on number of kids you may conceive before attracting the attention of social services is 9. Have more than 6 children, and your membership in the middle class is revoked.

AGE 31: MAKE A DOOMED ATTEMPT TO STAY IN SHAPE

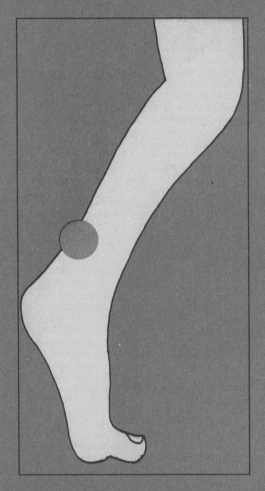

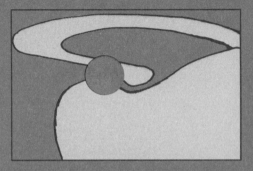

Shoulder dislocation

Upon excessive twisting or rotation, traumatic anterior (or posterior) dislocation of the shoulder may occur, with the humerus popping out of the glenohumeral joint, causing damage to the tissue and/or nerves. An X-ray is required before forcing the shoulder back into place under appropriate medical supervision. The arm will then need to be held in a sling until the healing process has occurred.

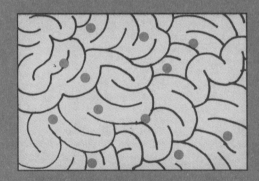

Achilles tendinitis

The Achilles tendon connects the Gastrocnemius muscle to the Calcaneus, and can become inflamed when placed under excessive stress through overuse. Collagen degeneration may also occur, resulting in tendinitis. To treat, massage with ice, and tape the Achilles tendon to take the strain off. Taking glucosamine supplements will also help. Achilles tendon rupture will require surgery.

Inguinal hernia

Inguinal hernias are lumps that emerge when part of the bowels leak into the groin area, often as a result of heavy lifting or other unusual strain on the abdominal muscles. Wearing a truss may soothe discomfort in the short term, but surgery is usually required to prevent the hernia from becoming strangulated and leading to gangrene or peritonitis.

The early thirties are a critical time for the human body. Either you can let yourself go, particularly if you've just started a family, or you can strain every sinew to hold on to your youthful body for a few more years at least. Here is how to treat the injuries that you will inevitably incur.

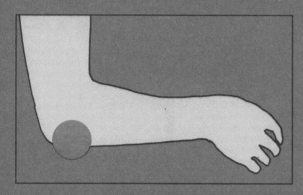

Tennis elbow

Repeated arm motions without proper stretching may cause a fraying of the elbow's tendons (aka "tennis elbow"), which in some cases is accompanied by calcification of the lateral epicondyle. Treatment involves rest and cortisone injections, progressing to arthroscopic surgery, with two small incisions under general anesthetic.

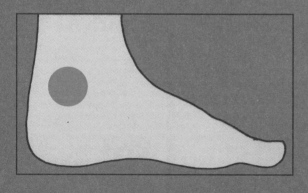

Sprained ankle

Sprained ankles are usually caused by involuntary inversion of the foot, and in most cases are characterized by damage to one or several of three lateral ligaments: the Anterior Talofibular, the Posterior Talofibular, and, more rarely, the Talocalcaneofibular. Treatment should initially consist of Rest, the application of Ice, Compression and Elevation (the R.I.C.E. method). Lengthy physiotherapy may also be required.

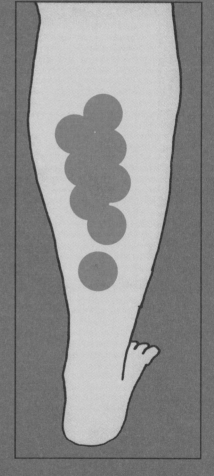

Muscle cramp

Cramp of the calf muscles may occur in athletes training harder than they are accustomed to. The exact cause is still unknown, but stretching and massage may help alleviate the condition. Warning: severe cramp may tear the muscle fibers apart. Do not massage at this stage, as it will increase the internal muscle bleeding and exacerbate the injury!

AGE 32: TURN INTO A WORKAHOLIC

Follow this 12-month plan.

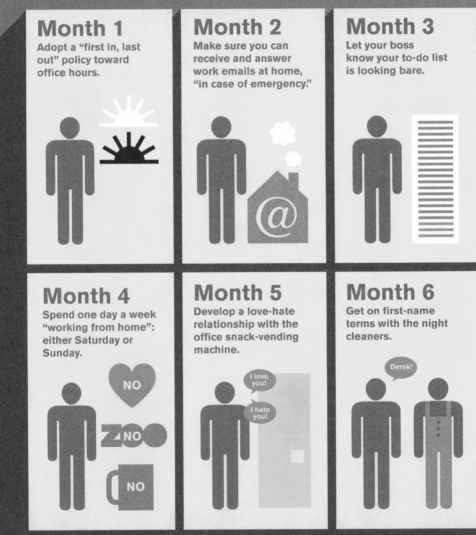

Month 1
Adopt a "first in, last out" policy toward office hours.

Month 2
Make sure you can receive and answer work emails at home, "in case of emergency."

Month 3
Let your boss know your to-do list is looking bare.

Month 4
Spend one day a week "working from home": either Saturday or Sunday.

Month 5
Develop a love-hate relationship with the office snack-vending machine.

Month 6
Get on first-name terms with the night cleaners.

By now, your role as an economic agent should begin to take precedence over your private life. This is difficult to accept for many, but if you manage the change gradually, you and those around you will hardly notice the transition.

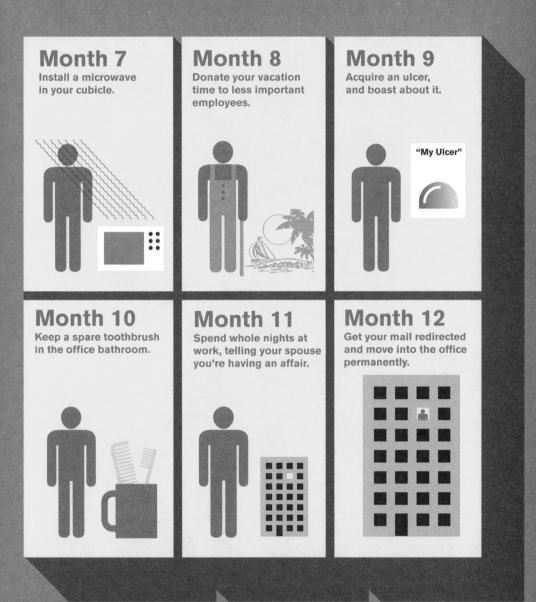

Month 7
Install a microwave in your cubicle.

Month 8
Donate your vacation time to less important employees.

Month 9
Acquire an ulcer, and boast about it.

"My Ulcer"

Month 10
Keep a spare toothbrush in the office bathroom.

Month 11
Spend whole nights at work, telling your spouse you're having an affair.

Month 12
Get your mail redirected and move into the office permanently.

AGE 33: LIVE THE NUCLEAR FAMILY DREAM

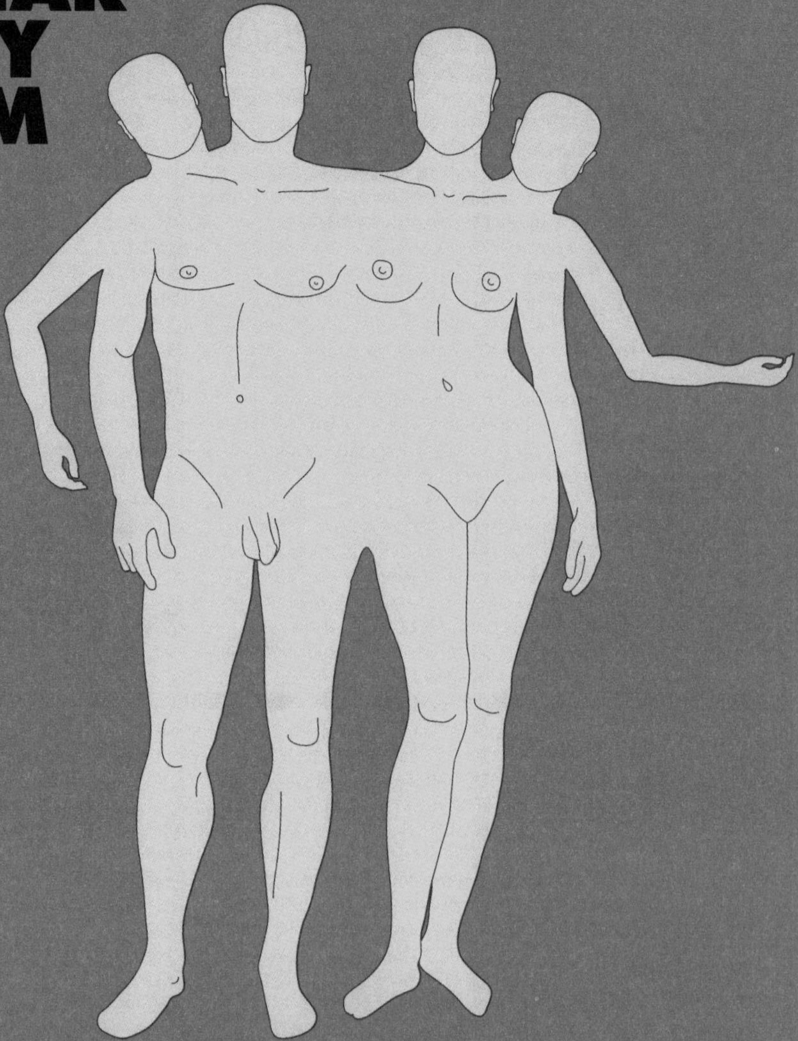

By 33, you should be married with a child or two (ideally 2.4, the statistical norm). Your family unit is the basis of any stable and wholesome society. Celebrate by applying to be surgically fused together, as shown in the medical diagram above.

We, the .... family,

hereby rejoice in our status as a nuclear family, proclaim our desire
to forever be united, and wish to formally apply for surgical fusion
(or "siamesation"). This is how we would like to see it turn out, please.

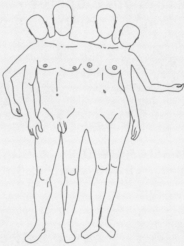

Signed and dated:

Nuclear family Dad: ....

Nuclear family Mom: ....

Nuclear family Child 1: ....

Nuclear family Child 2: ....

Nuclear family Child 0.4: ....

AGE 34: WRITE THE NOVEL THAT IS IN YOU

"She doesn't *look* 18," mused Pope John Paul III as he popped the last Viagra.

As he tasted the human, Emperor Zorg was reminded of chicken, a favorite dish on his planet.

Sheikh Abdullah strongly suspected his fourth wife had killed the other three, although he couldn't prove it—yet.

Nowhere in the 747 manual were pilots specifically warned against looping the loop, thought Captain Polizzio, preparing his defense.

In today's youth-obsessed world, success doesn't count if it comes after 40. At 34, there's still time to try and become rich and famous, and one of the easiest ways is to write a bestselling novel. All it takes is a pen and paper, a dictionary, and a bright idea for a plot. Here are some first lines to help you get started.

My mother could never tell me the exact date I was born, for she was drunk as a skunk at the time.

The time machine had given Professor Needleheim a throbbing migraine, and the sight of two pterodactyls humping a mere ten yards away was hardly helping.

After 76 years of trying, Mildred had finally lost her virginity.

The meteorite struck at 5:58 a.m., instantly wiping out all life on Earth.

AGE 35: SCRATCH YOUR SEVEN-YEAR ITCH

"Steve"

"My wife Laura and I were growing apart. Well, we'd been married seven years, you know what they say. Anyway, I had an affair with her sister Kathleen. We were drunk and one thing led to another. Laura came back from yoga early one night and found us together. Initially she was mad, but then it turned out she'd been getting friendly with MY brother Jerry. So we made up and our marriage is stronger than ever. Hell, now we all laugh about it!"

7-year itch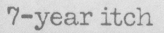

"Lucia"

"In those days, Scott was traveling a lot for work. I'm not saying that to excuse things but you know, I got lonely. I knew I still had a year to go before the seven-year itch, but hey I figured, what's one year? Little did I know. Anyway, he found out through the neighbors that our gardener Ramon was spending a little too much time indoors. He hired a private eye, and next thing I knew he'd filed for divorce. Now I'm back to waiting tables, meanwhile he hasn't even fired Ramon."

6-year itch

At 35, you are meant to have been married for seven years, so it's time to have that affair with your secretary, the milkman, a neighbor or other suitable candidate. Handled correctly, this needn't destroy your marriage, at least not in the short term. Caution: for biological reasons, it is imperative that you have the affair seven years after marriage exactly, as the following case studies make clear.

"Brian"

"I knew I'd left my affair a bit late. We'd just celebrated our eighth-year anniversary, and on a business trip I ended up having a one-night stand with this hot sales rep from Nevada. My boss saw her come out of my room and fired me on the spot. When I explained what happened to my wife, she kicked me out of the house and changed the locks. Now I'm living in a hostel, and to top it all I've just noticed this lumpy growth in my groin. Do you know a cheap doctor?"

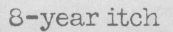8-year itch

"Amanda"

"Let me see, well first there was Troy who I met at the wedding party, then there was the bartender on our honeymoon, then the real estate agent, because, you know, I was the one viewing the houses, then I've always had a thing for builders, so that was that episode, and then when I got pregnant I was feeling unsexy, and so naturally I turned to Dr. Johnson my gynecologist, such strong hands! So far, my husband Mikey hasn't noticed though, what a sweetheart!"

1-year itch

AGE 36: BURDEN YOUR KIDS WITH UNREASONABLE EXPECTATIONS

When Daddy was your age, he was much taller. You'll never become president if you don't eat your broccoli. "And they lived happily ever after." You want to marry a prince too, don't you? Pray every night, and nothing bad will ever happen to you. Mommy and Daddy fell in love at first sight! Yes, 2 plus 2 does equal 4! Ohmigod, she's a genius!

As a parent, one of your key duties is to instill a proper sense of ambition in your kids. How else will they cope with the nerve-racking grind of advanced capitalist society? Don't be afraid to step over the mark: better too much ambition than too little. Here are some verbal techniques that will help.

Mommy loves you very much, and so does everyone in the world. Your father was a general, and so was your grandfather, and his father before him. "New York Yan-kees." One day you'll play for them, boy. The violin is very easy to master, you'll see. We called you Albert, after a famous scientist. Boys will love you if you're comfortable with yourself.

AGE 37: HAVE AN EARLY MIDLIFE CRISIS

Arzfeld & Schwartz Divorce Lawyers
Hourly fee $200 (down from $250) + initial consultation free of charge.

Autorent Worldwide
Special Discount: 10% off official price on weekly rate for Porsche Carrera.

It's best to get the midlife crisis out of your system while you're still young enough to enjoy it. The authors have put together a very affordable package, which will help you through this difficult time without breaking the bank.

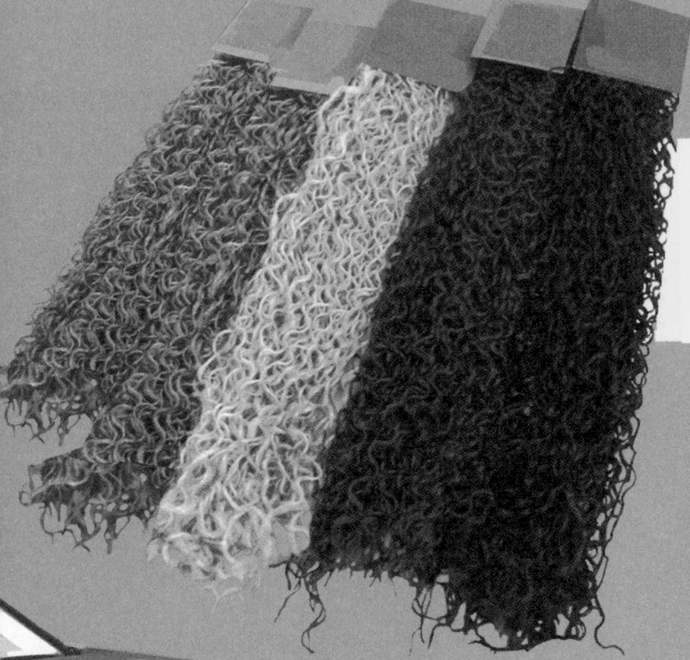

Flavio's
Hair Salon
Coloring $90 (women)
$70 (men).

BIG 1

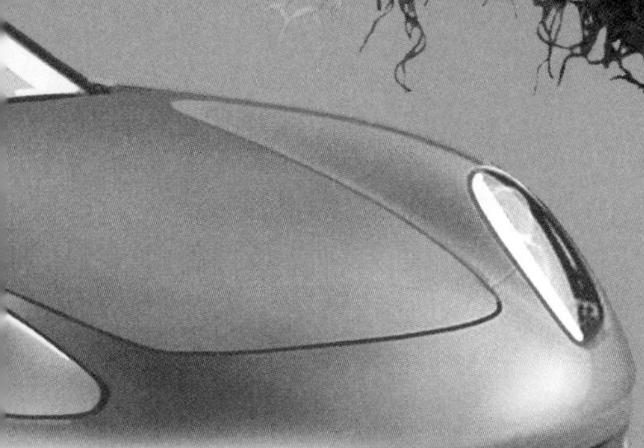

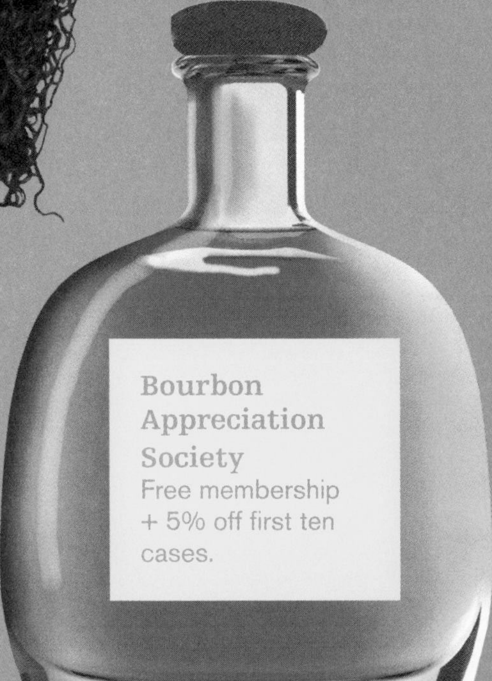

Bourbon
Appreciation
Society
Free membership
+ 5% off first ten
cases.

See www.thiswebsitewillchangeyourlife.com for details!

AGE 38: CLIMB THE CAREER LADDER

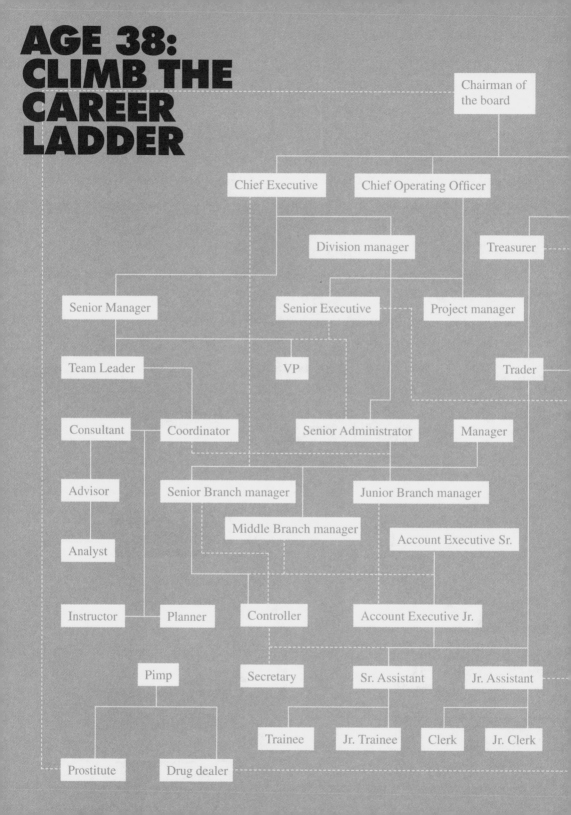

At the age of 38, you must focus on your prospects,
or be forever doomed to middle management.
Here is the hierarchy of career titles in Western society.
Use it to plan your way to the top.

AGE 39:
DENY
YOUR AGE

Last chance *VIP Card*

Name...

Address..

....

....

....

....

Photo

Attention venue-owners! The bearer is 39 and thus only has one year or less
in which to frequent your facilities without appearing ridiculous. Please
make them feel welcome and refrain from mentioning their age. Thank you.

The last year of your thirties should be marked by apparent denial. Youth officially ends at 40, so use your thirty-ninth year to act out any culturally "youth-exclusive" activities for the very last time. To help, we provide a VIP card which recognizes your status and gives you priority entrance to a range of youth venues.

Clubs

601 Club (16th St, New York)
Christy's (Lenox Ave, New York)
Kink Lounge (Sunset Blvd, Los Angeles)
Planet 69 (Walnut St, Philadelphia)
The Cojones (Revere St, Houston)
Bankrupt (Pike Place, Seattle)
The Kabul Klub (Church St, San Francisco)
Frantic (University Ave, Minneapolis)
The Asylum (Central Ave, Albuquerque)
Mook (4th Ave, Tucson)

Bars

Retox (45 Cleeve St, Detroit)
644 (Kapahulu Ave, Honolulu)
Strontium (Sullivan St, New York)
Guantanamo Beach (Stanton St, New York)
The Riot (S Lamar, Austin)
The AK-47 (N Wells St, Chicago)
Atari Room (Beacon St, Boston)
The Colonel Kurtz (India St, San Diego)
Shock&Awe (W Layton Ave, Milwaukee)
The Cliché (6th St, Los Angeles)

Fashion

Urban Hype (Biscayne Blvd, Miami)
Fashionista (Canal St, New York)
ScarSkate (Bandera St, San Antonio)
Def Street (Malcolm X Blvd, New York)
Phat Couture (Bagley St, Detroit)
Forever 18 (Lexington St, Baltimore)
Miss Tery (Lafayette St, New York)
Project XXX (Charles St, Boston)
Bodycount (Connecticut Ave, Washington)
Wiggawear (S Figueroa, Los Angeles)

Electric guitar shops

McDermott's Guitar Shop (5th Ave, Seattle)
Guitar City (Camp Bowie Blvd, Forth Worth)
Stratocasterati (Broad St, Philadelphia)
JB Guitars (87th St, New York)
Strings on Sunset (Sunset Blvd, Los Angeles)
Phoenix Music (E Van Buren St, Phoenix)
Backstage Bass (Old Pueblo Rd, El Paso)
Stairway To Heaven (N Lee St, Chicago)
The Strum Store (N Meridian, Indianapolis)
Guitar Gurus (North High St, Columbus)

Gigs

Voodoo Mansion (Adams Ave, Chicago)
The Metal Factory (Venice Rd, Toledo)
The Casbah (Santa Monica Blvd, Los Angeles)
Trash Towers (Washington Ave, New York)
Franklin's (Franklin St, New York)
The Blood Shed (Broadway, Nashville)
Dive Central (Ingersoll Ave, Des Moines)
No Man's Land (Forbes Ave, Pittsburgh)
Sing-Sing (Mason St, San Francisco)
The Freebase (N Mentor Ave, Los Angeles)

Drug dealers

Tony (Washington Square Park, New York)
Manuel (The Strip, Las Vegas)
Jerry (South Central, Los Angeles)
Larry (North Beach, San Francisco)
JJ (Queens, New York)
Jimmy (Miami Beach, Miami)
Pablo (14 St, Miami)
Daz (Downtown, Cleveland)
Freddie (Port area, Cincinnati)
Scarface (Harlem, New York)

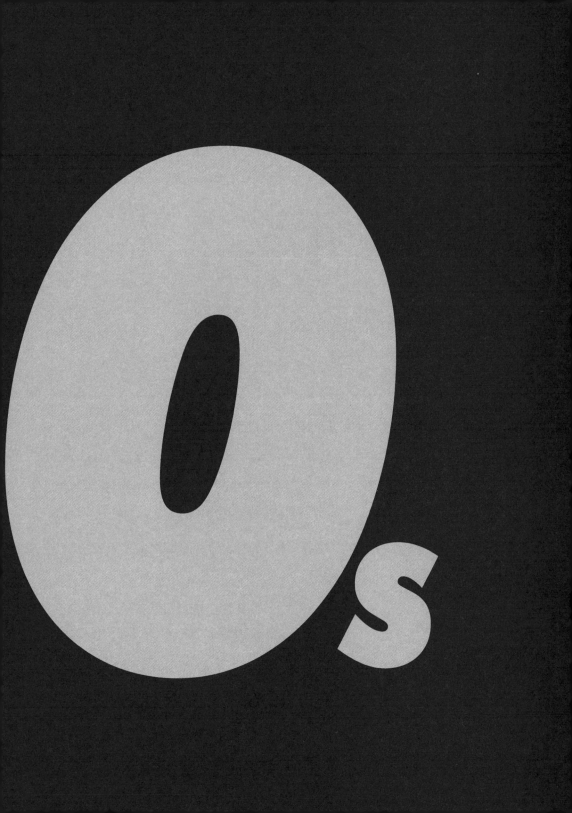

AGE 40: GROW UP

"Bach"
1685-1750

Top hit: Brandenburg Concertos
Famous for: writing obscene
number of works, fathering
obscene number of children
Grown-up gravitas: 9/10

Hum sample in the elevator:

"Mozart"
1756-1791

Top hit: Requiem
Famous for: being child
prodigy, featuring in crowd-
pleasing Hollywood film
Grown-up gravitas: 4/10

Sing sample in the shower:

In our culture, 40 is a milestone, a line in the sand between youth and maturity. At 40, you are incontestably a grown-up, with rights, responsibilities, and the obligation to maintain a certain gravitas at all times. Listening to classical music on a regular basis will assist you, and indeed is a prerequisite of grown-upness.

"Beethoven"
1770-1827

Top hit: 5th Symphony
Famous for: unkempt head of hair, deafness, being generally tormented
Grown-up gravitas: 7/10

"Wagner"
1813-1883

Top hit: The Ring
Famous for: limited sense of humor, proto-fascist leanings, unsavory daughter-in-law
Grown-up gravitas: 8/10

AGE 41: BEGIN THERAPY

Possible Issues

1. WOMB

Draw your position in the womb
(if you cannot remember, ask your mother):

Ex.

Ok   Not ok

2. INNER CHILD

Sketch a rough portrait
of your inner child:

Ex.

Good   Naughty
inner child!   inner child!

The first forty years of your life will have turned you into a tangled mass of neuroses and repressed longings. Coupled with the realization that you're no longer young, this should precipitate a nervous breakdown of some severity. You will need expensive therapy for the foreseeable future; try to work out the source of any "issues" yourself below, to help the therapist get a head start on your case.

3. RECOVERED MEMORIES

Write down your main repressed memories. If you're finding it difficult to recover them, try using one of the random words below as a trigger:

....
....
....
....
....
....
....
....
....
....

"Uncle" "Secret" "Play" "No!" "Shush" "Hurts" "Don't Tell Daddy Or Mommy Now"

4. SEXUAL IDENTITY

Answer these questions as honestly as you can:

	Yes	No
Heterosexuals: Are you secretly gay?	☐	☐
Homosexuals: Are you secretly hetero?	☐	☐

Both:
Do you have any sexual urges repressed deep within your subconscious?

Yes ☐　No ☐　Don't know ☐

5. PARENTS

Draw your mother and father:

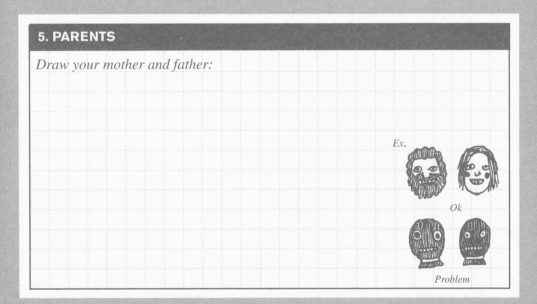

Ex.

Ok

Problem

AGE 42: MOVE TO THE SUBURBS

Life should be a little exciting, unpredictable, dangerous even. But not forever. At 42, it is time for you to settle down to a more sedate existence: suburbia beckons. Use the following checklist to make sure your future suburb meets all the requirements.

Suburb Checklist

Fresh air ☐
No traffic gridlock ☐
No getting mugged after dark ☐
No threatening youths ☐
No "ghettoblasters" on public transport ☐
No "breakdancing" in the streets ☐
No "graffiti" on the walls ☐
No Bloods ☐
No Crips ☐
No gangs of any description ☐
No crack cocaine pipes lying around ☐
No used condoms for toddlers to pick up ☐
No serial killers on the loose ☐
No drunken tramps ☐
No drive-by shootings ☐
No drug dealers in building hallways ☐

AGE 43: JOIN THE SWINGING SCENE

Box of Tide in the window: Husband away traveling on business.

Outdoor light on during day: We are naked and tied up: please walk in.

Purple begonias in flower bed: Cross-dressing husband needs good spanking.

Suburbia is a great place for raising kids, as well as for some unwholesome sexual experimentation. There's not much else to do, so get to know your neighbors in the biblical sense. Here are the secret codes used to indicate proclivities.

Bedroom shutter half open:
Hard-core S&M bondage fans only.

Milk bottle upside down:
Homemade pornos now casting.

Lawn mown in East-West pattern:
Seeking mature ladies for threesome.

AGE 44: ENJOY THE FINER THINGS IN LIFE

Champagne

$5 off a magnum!

VINTAGES COVERED:
1982, 1983, 1985, 1986, 1988, 1995, 1998, 2001

Retailer: Contact the authors for discount code.

FOIE GRAS

$20 off the 2nd kilo bought!

(GRADE 1 ONLY)

Retailer: Contact the authors for discount code.

CASHMERE

10% off all cashmere sweaters!

Pashmina two-ply weave

Retailer: Contact the authors for discount code.

Lobster

4 for the price of **3**!

FEMALE EUROPEAN "BRETON" ONLY

Retailer: Contact the authors for discount code.

At 44, you can afford to take it easy. Relax and focus on the material comforts that middle-aged affluence provides. You've earned it: so sit back and enjoy the fruits of your labor. Here are some coupons to redeem at any luxury retail outlet near you.

Cigars

5 extra

for each box of 25!

COHIBA ESPLENDIDOS OR ROBUSTOS

Retailer: Contact the authors for discount code.

DIAMONDS

5%

off any ring or necklace!

2 karat or more

Retailer: Contact the authors for discount code.

CAVIAR

15% off

a 700g pot of Beluga!

20% off Osteria or Sevruga!

Retailer: Contact the authors for discount code.

Fur

33%

off any fur garment!

FURS COVERED:

Chinchilla, Beaver, Ermine, Mink

Retailer: Contact the authors for discount code.

AGE 45: ADOPT A THIRD WORLD ORPHAN

1. Ethiopia
GDP per capita: $700
Life expectancy at birth: 48
Prospects for orphans: Grim
Cuteness of orphans: High
Guilt trip: 9/10
Contact: Children and Youth
Affairs Office, Ministry of
Labor and Social Affairs, Kirkos
Kifle Ketema, Kebele 18, Kazanchis,
Addis Ababa.

2. Bolivia
GDP per capita: $2,300
Life expectancy at birth: 65
Prospects for orphans: Remote
Cuteness of orphans: Medium-high
Guilt trip: 8.5/10
Contact: Viceministerio de La
Juventud, Niñez y Tercera Edad,
Edificio El Condor, 1 St Floor,
Suite 101, Batallon Colorados
St. #24, La Paz.

3. Romania
GDP per capita: $6,900
Life expectancy at birth: 71
Prospects for orphans: Bleak
Cuteness of orphans: Average
Guilt trip: 7/10
Contact: Suspended until further
notice due to child trafficking.

**Adoption
Hit Parade**

Your middle-class guilt trip should hit you round about now. What better way to deal with it than giving everything to someone who has nothing? Adopting a third world orphan is the perfect antidote to a materialistic bourgeois lifestyle. But which third world country is most deserving?

4. China

GDP per capita: $5,800
Life expectancy at birth: 72
Prospects for orphans: Poor
Cuteness of orphans: Quite high
Guilt trip: 6.5/10
Contact: Center for Adoption Affairs
7 Baiguang Rd, Zhongmin Building,
Xuanwu District, Beijing 100053.

5. Vietnam

GDP per capita: $2,400
Life expectancy at birth: 70
Prospects for orphans: Medium-bleak
Cuteness of orphans: Above average
Guilt trip: 6/10
Contact: Dept of International Adoptions
Central Building, Suite 108, 31 Hai Ba Trung, Hanoi.

AGE 46: DIVORCE MESSILY

Cut out one of the following excuses and leave it under your spouse's pillow.

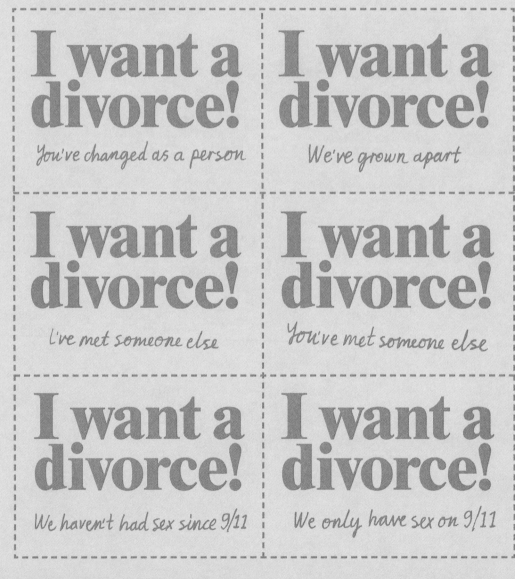

I want a divorce!
You've changed as a person

I want a divorce!
We've grown apart

I want a divorce!
I've met someone else

I want a divorce!
You've met someone else

I want a divorce!
We haven't had sex since 9/11

I want a divorce!
We only have sex on 9/11

46 is a sensible age at which to divorce. You still have time to remarry. Your kids are in their early teenage years, a particularly vulnerable stage. You have been together for a decent length of time, so you'll have common possessions to fight over. And you can afford proper lawyers. All the ingredients for a messy divorce are there. All you need now is a good excuse!

I want a divorce!
Your crack cocaine habit has gotten out of control

I want a divorce!
It's what my other family wants

I want a divorce!
My sexual orientation has changed

I want a divorce!
Your sexual orientation has changed

I want a divorce!
God has told me so

I want a divorce!
I hate everything about you

AGE 47: ABANDON THE AMERICAN DREAM

The American Dream

*One day,
you will retire a
millionaire, through
sheer hard work
and determination.*

The Russian Dream

*One day, you will
retire a millionaire,
through nepotism
and corruption of
state funds.*

The Saudi Dream

*One day,
you will retire a
millionaire after
striking oil in your
backyard.*

The Italian Dream

*One day,
you will retire and
be supported by
your countless
grandchildren.*

There comes a time when you must face the sad facts of life: unless you have made your millions and bought your yacht by now, you probably never will. But don't despair: ditch the American Dream and pursue one of the more attainable dreams below.

The British Dream

One day, you will retire with a nice pension and live in the countryside.

The French Dream

One day, you will retire with a nice pension or you will riot until the government falls.

The World Dream

One day, you will have saved enough money to retire.

The Ethiopian Dream

One day, you will reach retirement age.

AGE 48:
FIGHT
THE FLAB

At 48 or thereabouts, you face a stark choice. Either you fight your body fat's expansion plans, or you let yourself go. This is what you will look like within a few years if you give in. Cut out and stick on your fridge to help ward off temptation.

AGE 49:
BE ABDUCTED
BY ALIENS

 **LIE #1** The human male's penis is able to emit a powerful laser beam, which kills both his target and himself, rather like a bee's sting.

 **LIE #2** The moon is in fact an anti-alien death star, due for imminent activation.

 LIE #3 The most desirable human beings to attempt intercourse with are those with "gonorrhea."

LIE #4 The Roswell alien is still alive and kept in a big jar in the Oval Office.

 LIE #5 Providing the returned abductees with lots of human "money" helps the amnesia process.

This happens to everyone at some point. But 49 is the most common age, as aliens prefer to abduct our society's decision-makers. Make your abduction more interesting by lying to the aliens in your interrogation. Confuse them enough, and you may even postpone their invasion.

LIE #6
Our planet's leaders all drive pick-up trucks. Make them priority abduction targets.

LIE #7
Using the anal probe on humans is counterproductive as it only increases our powers tenfold.

LIE #8
The French are not human, but from a planet riva to yours.

LIE #9
When E.T. was here, he wouldn't stop bitching about the rest of you guys.

LIE #10
Men are from Mars, women are from Venus.

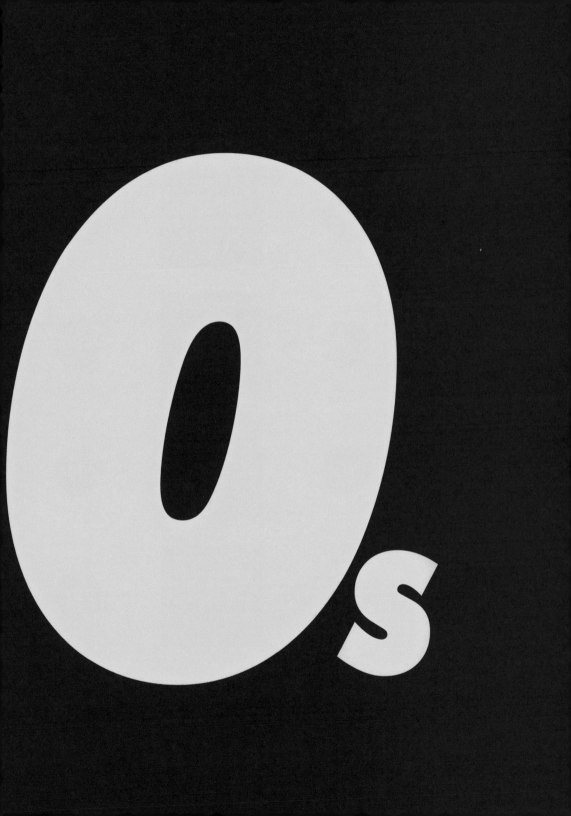

AGE 50: BECOME RIGHT-WING

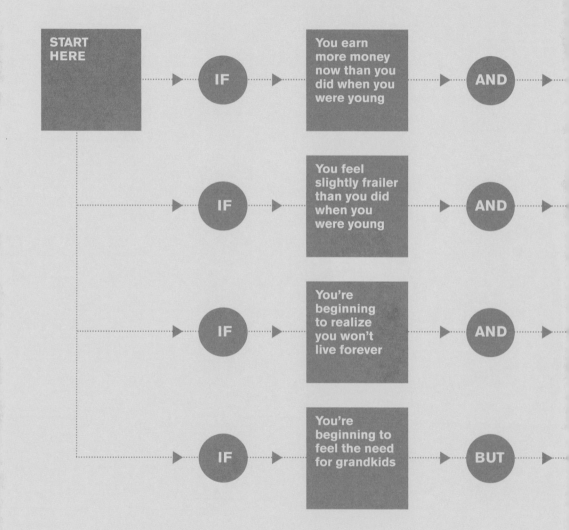

START HERE → IF → You earn more money now than you did when you were young → AND →

IF → You feel slightly frailer than you did when you were young → AND →

IF → You're beginning to realize you won't live forever → AND →

IF → You're beginning to feel the need for grandkids → BUT →

DAMN HIPPIES...

After half a century on earth, even the commiest peacenik veers sharply to the right. There is nothing wrong with this, and in fact it is an entirely rational, logical outcome of middle age. Let us guide you through it with this simple flow chart.

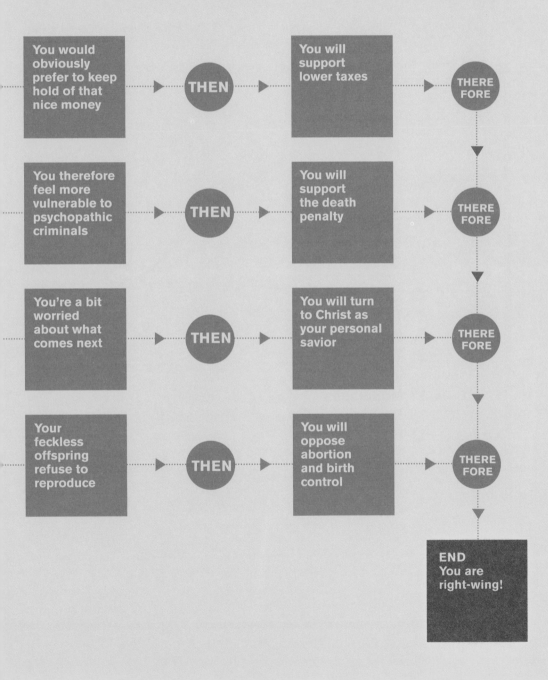

AGE 51: GO THROUGH THE MENOPAUSE

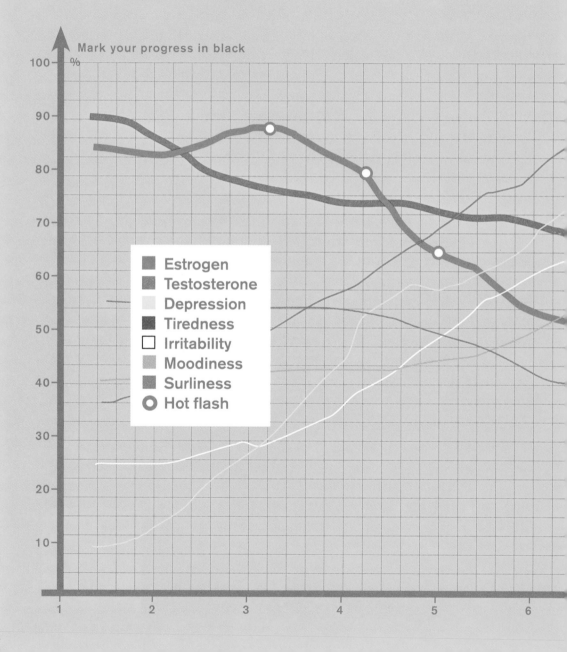

Mark your progress in black

%

Legend:
- Estrogen
- Testosterone
- Depression
- Tiredness
- Irritability
- Moodiness
- Surliness
- ○ Hot flash

The menopause affects both women and men these days, causing physical and psychological trauma almost as upsetting as that of adolescence. Try and minimize this by aiming for a steady, managed decline in hormone levels. The graph below should give you the idea.

<u>Follow it faithfully, and you will enjoy a smooth menopause.</u>

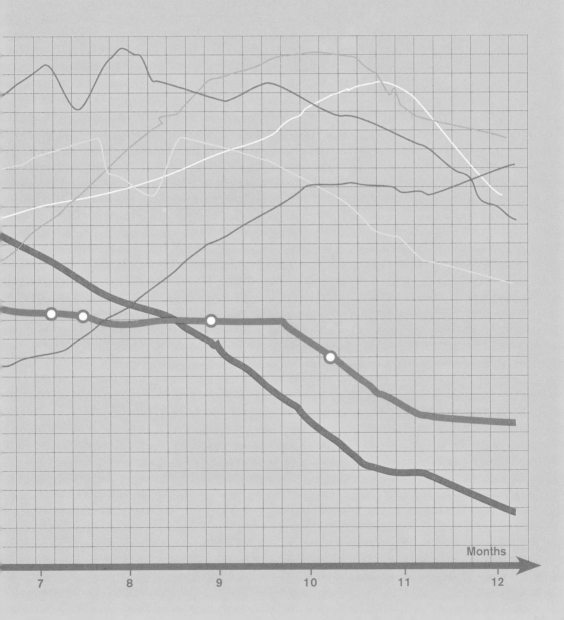

Months

7   8   9   10   11   12

AGE 52: SWIM WITH DOLPHINS

Do not swim toward the dolphin.

Do not get between a hungry dolphin and its plankton.

Do not touch the dolphin inappropriately, even if it makes the first move.

Do not try to swim faster than the dolphin.

At 52, the "midlife-crisis crisis" strikes. Have you dealt with your midlife crisis successfully? Have you coped better than your peers with the realization that ageing is inevitable? Probably not. To cure the resulting depression, there is a time-honored 100% natural solution: swimming with dolphins. Here are the basic safety guidelines.

Do not communicate with the dolphin except through sonar.

Do not pee in the sea, the dolphin lives there.

Do not let the dolphin-happiness overwhelm you to the point where you drown.

If the dolphin tries to eat you, it's a shark. Swim away.

AGE 53: DEVELOP AN UNHEALTHY ADDICTION TO GOLF

A:

Hot...

Like some obscure masonic ritual, the appeal of golf is kept from us until we reach a certain age: 53. From now on, golf will be with you for the rest of your life, eventually becoming the source of your deepest thrills. To help effect the transition, focus on picture A. Once you're suitably aroused, close your eyes, hold those feelings, then open your eyes and stare at picture. B. Eventually, this technique will help you transfer your feelings of erotic gratification from sex to golf.

B:

Hotter!

AGE 54: JOIN ALCOHOLICS ANONYMOUS

Hi, my name is ...
and I'm an alcoholic.

What drove me to drink was:
my wife / husband / kids / job.

I first realized I had a problem when:
I woke up shaking /
I woke up in the gutter /
I woke up still drunk.

I drink to get drunk/
I drink to forget /
I've forgotten why I drink.

My alcohol of choice is:
expensive French red wine /
cheap American bourbon /
there's different kinds?

No life story is complete without a battle against the bottle. Your drink problem can last a lifetime, but 54 is the age at which it should come to a crux and you should seek help. Call your local AA group, and attend your first meeting. You may use this short preprepared speech to soothe your nerves:

My **worst drinking incident involved:**
paramedics / the police /
the armed forces.

My **liver:**
has **been damaged / needs replacing /**
has crawled out of my
body of its own accord.

I am here because:
my spouse threatened to divorce /
my family and friends made me /
hang on, where's the
alcohol you promised?

Thank you for listening /
Thank you for sharing /
Thank you for all featuring in my
local gossip column tomorrow morning.

AGE 55: PUT YOUR PARENTS IN A HOME

BEST
FOR
YOU

No more forced viewings of History Channel marathons.

Unencumbered weekends in Palm Springs.

Expensive dinners for two at latest restaurants.

Plenty of room for post-50 sexual fulfilment.

The security of knowing your folks are getting cared for by professionals.

A guilt-free existence.

A life free from constant judgment.

One visit a year.

For years, your parents have supported you in all your endeavors. They have been a huge influence on your life, making you the person you are today. Thank them by parking them in a cheap rest home while you get out and enjoy yourself. If they protest, simply remind them that this is "the best thing for all of us." Insisting that "you've had your day" may also help.

Medication delivered in handy paper cup.

A window to watch the squirrels from.

Denture-conscious mush in a bevy of pleasing colors.

Unwanted advances from shifty night staff employees.

The strong probability of being misdiagnosed by untrained imbeciles.

Paper diapers.

Arts and crafts every Thursday.

One visit a year.

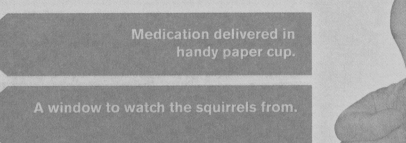

BEST
FOR
THEM

AGE 56: HAVE PLASTIC SURGERY

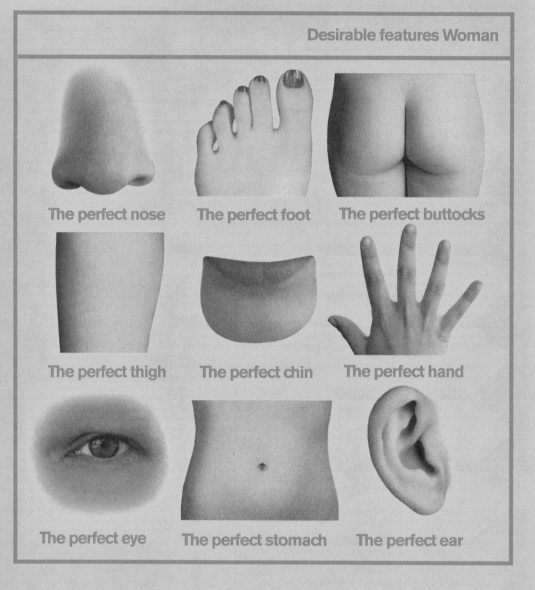

Desirable features Woman

The perfect nose The perfect foot The perfect buttocks

The perfect thigh The perfect chin The perfect hand

The perfect eye The perfect stomach The perfect ear

Total to pay:...

Plastic surgery is one of the few treats of advancing age. You should wait until you need it, but not so late that you miss out on the accompanying benefits (younger lovers, jealous siblings, incredulous colleagues). 56 is about right. Here is a reference guide to the perfect body parts. Circle the ones you require and hand to your surgeon.

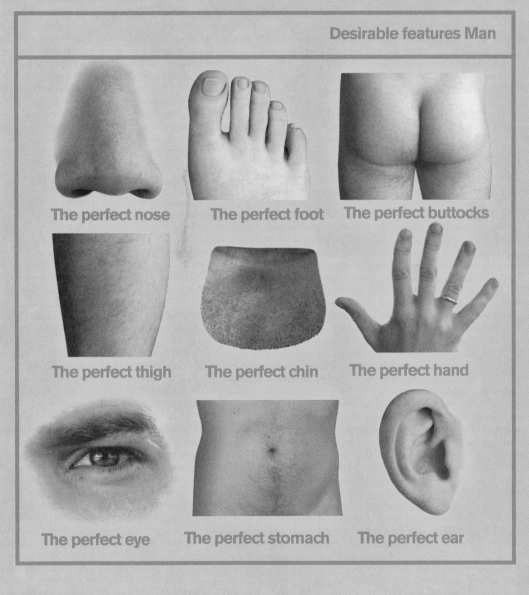

Desirable features Man

The perfect nose   The perfect foot   The perfect buttocks

The perfect thigh   The perfect chin   The perfect hand

The perfect eye   The perfect stomach   The perfect ear

Total to pay:..

AGE 57: MARRY OFF YOUR CHILDREN

Marrying off your daughter

Acceptable ☐
Not acceptable ☐

Acceptable ☐
Not acceptable ☐

Acceptable ☐
Not acceptable ☐

Acceptable ☐
Not acceptable ☐

By your late fifties, you have proudly raised your kids, bringing them up in the harsh modern world, steering them through the thorny thickets of adolescence, and helping them develop a healthy sense of selfhood. Now it's time to get rid of the little parasites. Decide on a level of looks you consider worthy of them and arrange a marriage, using this criteria chart.

Marrying off your son

Acceptable ☐
Not acceptable ☐

Acceptable ☐
Not acceptable ☐

Acceptable ☐
Not acceptable ☐

Acceptable ☐
Not acceptable ☐

AGE 58: TURN INTO YOUR PARENTS

However hard you try to fight it, whatever attempts you make to the contrary, and no matter how much you protest it will never happen to you, one fine morning you will wake up and realize you have become your parents. This is a genetically-driven process: every niggling habit of theirs, every small-minded view, every physical tic is encoded into your DNA, programmed to emerge round about now. It is vain to fight it. Instead, rejoice! One day, your kids too will turn into you...

Mark the moment!
I turned into my parents on the
.... / .... 20.............
at............o´clock exactly.

AGE 59: WIN THE RAT RACE

At 59, you should be reaching the pinnacle of your career: chairman, CEO, head nurse, captain astronaut, whatever. Take a moment to record the damage you have wreaked on your way to the top.

❶ Colleague whom you forced to resign:...

❷ Colleague whom you demoted:...

❸ Colleague whom you fired:...

❹ Colleague whom you had fired:..

❺ Colleague whom you trampled on:..

❻ Colleague whom you ate alive:...

❼ Colleague whom you ate for breakfast:...

❽ Colleague whom you humiliated in meetings:.....................................

❾ Colleague whom you bullied:..

❿ Colleague who jumped out the window because of you:.....................

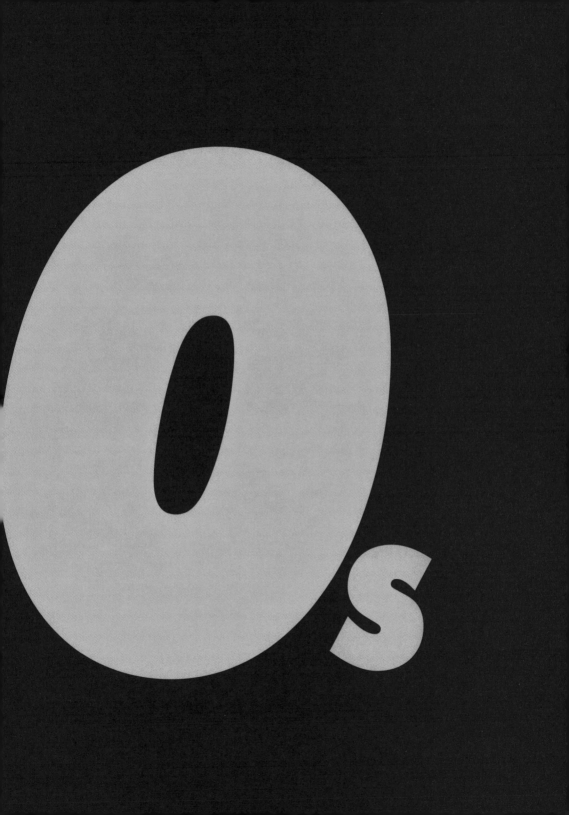

AGE 60: UNDERGO A SPIRITUAL REBIRTH

Religion	History	Beliefs	Sacred text	Logo
BUDDHISM	Founded by Siddartha Gautama (the Buddha) in the 5th century BC in what is now Nepal, Buddhism spread across much of Asia in the centuries following his death.	There is no God; we go through a succession of reincarnations, with our past actions influencing our next life. The cycle can be halted by reaching enlightenment (nirvana), essentially through meditation and the Middle Way.	The Tri-Pitaka.	
hinduism	Hinduism is one of the world's oldest religions, originating over 3000 years ago near the river Indus, with complex roots and no single human founder.	There is a universal God or soul called Brahman, who is also expressed in the form of deities such as Krishna, Vishnu, Shiva, and Rama. Life is a great cycle of birth, death and rebirth, governed by Karma, the law of cause and effect.	The Bhagavad Gita, The Upanishads.	
paganism	Modern paganism covers most of the ancestral pre-monotheistic religions of the world, from Celtic druidry to Native American shamanism.	Nature and Mother Earth are spiritual, and are to be respected and worshipped, often in the guise of individual gods. The divine in nature has a strong feminine side, linked to the renewal and rebirth of the seasons.	The Golden Bough (Sir James George Frazer).	
atheism	Atheism is a relatively recent creed. Although the Greeks hinted at it, it only really took off with the Enlightenment. In the 19th century, Darwin, Feuerbach and Nietzsche all contributed to its rapid spread. It is now the unofficial religion of the West.	There are no gods. Faith is mere superstition to comfort the feeble-minded and/or prop up oppressive power systems.	Thus Spake Zarathustra (Nietzsche).	$
islam	Founded by the Prophet Muhammad in the 7th century after a direct revelation from Allah, Islam swiftly spread both west (all the way to Spain) and east (all the way to China).	Allah is the one and only God. Islam was revealed to humanity by Muhammad, Allah's last prophet. We must obey the Qu'ran and surrender ourselves to Allah.	The Qu'ran.	
JUDAISM	Judaism was founded 3500 years ago by Abraham and Moses—who led the Jewish people from Egyptian captivity to the Promised Land of Israel. Judaism has since accompanied the Jewish people in their dramatic history of exiles, persecutions and other tribulations.	There is only one God. The Jews are his chosen people.	The Torah.	
CHRISTIANITY	Founded by Jesus Christ, persecuted and crucified by the Romans for his heretical views. Said to have risen from the dead. Word spread by his apostles, including Paul. Christians persecuted until Roman emperor Constantine converted in 312 CE.	Jesus is the son of God, sent by him to redeem humanity. He was crucified for our sins but rose from the dead to join God in heaven.	The Bible.	†

You are now 60, and should be reflecting on your purpose on this earth, the point of it all, and what will happen to you after you shuffle off your mortal coil. You may not believe in heaven and hell, but there's no harm in hedging your bets, just on the off-chance. Use our chart to determine which religion you wish to be reborn in.

Slogan	Rituals	Commitment level	Popular appeal	Your rating
"To avoid all that is evil, to cultivate what is good, to purify the mind."	These vary according to the different traditions, but meditation and some chanting are usually in order.	Medium. Risk of being reborn as a beetle of some description.	350 million adherents worldwide, and an increasing influence on the Western popular worldview.	10
"The mind of man is the root of both bondage and release."	Offerings to the Gods, recitation of the Vedas, oblations, chanting of mantras.	Medium to high, depending on your caste.	Big in India of course. Appeal elsewhere restricted by its deep integration into Indian society, and by the bewildering variety of subgods.	10
"The Earth is our Mother and we must take care of her."	Music, prayer, dance, conducted in sacred circles outdoors on hilltops, in caves, near large stones.	Medium-high. Requires a high tolerance of public ridicule and/or accusations of deviant sexual practices.	Limited. Although neo-paganism has seen a resurgence, partly fueled by the growth in ecological awareness, it is still a niche religion with a PR problem.	10
"God is dead."	May adopt watered-down versions of other religions' rituals (weddings, funerals, Christmas).	Used to involve being burnt at the stake. Now less risky.	Widespread. Most atheists are happy to just dismiss the whole religion thing, and hope like hell they don't turn out to be wrong.	10
"There is no God but Allah, and Muhammad is his messenger."	The five pillars of Islam are: 1) Shahada (declaration of faith) 2) Salat (prayer five times a day) 3) Zakat (giving to charity every year) 4) Sawm (fasting during Ramadan) 5) Hajj (pilgrimage to Mecca at least once in a lifetime).	High. Islam requires more visible worship than most religions.	Over a billion adherents make it the second most popular faith in the world. Also the fastest-growing.	10
"Hear O Israel, the Lord our God, the Lord is One."	Too numerous to detail.	High. Orthodox Judaism pervades everyday life.	Limited, as Judaism is not a proselytizing faith.	10
"Love Thy Neighbor As Thyself."	Baptism, Confirmation, Eucharist.	High in theory, variable in practice.	Most popular faith in the world, with over 2 billion followers.	10

At 61, it is time to stop looking on the bright side of things, and instead develop an unerring focus on the negative. Every cloud has a dark, cumulonimbal lining. Make it your mission to find it and broadcast it to those around you, as illustrated below.

❶ "Pesky kids!"
❷ "Air too hot!"
❸ "People too loud!"
❹ "Path too hard!"
❺ "Dangerous!"
❻ "Little hooligan!"
❼ "Cause allergies!"
❽ "Not mown!"
❾ "Shit on you!"
❿ "Too bright!"
⓫ "Risk of rain!"
⓬ "Polluted!"

AGE 62:
DO PRESCRIPTION
DRUGS

Combo: PROZAC + VIAGRA
Name: *Happy Pappy*
Pros: Warm glow,
recaptured youth
Cons: Detachment from
reality, heart attacks

Combo: PROZAC + XANAX
Name: *Momma's Little Helper*
Pros: Even temper,
permanent smiling
Cons: Valley of the Dolls issues

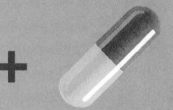

Combo: VICODIN + PAXIL
Name: *The Numbinator*
Pros: Complete lack of
pain in all forms
Cons: Doubting of
own existence

Combo: LIPITOR + ALLEGRA
Name: *Spring Cleaner*
Pros: Improved breathing
and blood flow
Cons: Occasional loss of
bowel control

Developing a healthy addiction to prescription drugs is a must, especially for anyone that's been in rehab. Now, these drugs may be legal, but they're certainly not boring, particularly if you mix them. Refer to this Combo Chart and you'll soon be awash in the soothing bliss of chemically-aided denial.

Combo: XANAX + PRILOSEC
Name: *Steady Eddie*
Pros: Clear-headed, heartburn-free thinking
Cons: Surreal numbness of extremities

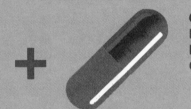

Combo: RITALIN + VALIUM
Name: *Hi-Ho (aka Ho-Hi)*
Pros: High-strung relaxation
Cons: Extremely mellow panic

Combo: ASPIRIN + PENICILLIN
Name: *Old Faithful*
Pros: Pain-free urination
Cons: Chalky aftertaste

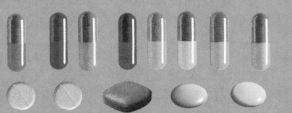

Combo:
Whatever is in the cabinet
Name: *Potpourri*
Pros: Surprise highs
Cons: Strong possibility of sudden death

AGE 63:
RUN FOR
OFFICE

There comes a time when every citizen feels the urge to play their part in the running of the community, in venerable Athenian statesman style. Fortunately, there are any number of offices you can get elected to, from State Senator to City Clerk, from District Attorney to Register of Wills. Some are more lowly than others, but all require you to file a nominating petition signed by a minimum number of voters in the first place. Start the ball rolling with this ready-made petition form.

I, ...
aged a very venerable 63,
am running for the office

of ....

In return for your support,
I promise you the following
favor when I get elected:
....
....
....
....

Please sign below to
support me, thank you!

Your name:......................................
Address:..
....

Signature:..

AGE 64:
SEE YOUR PAST
CATCH UP
WITH YOU

Crisis from your past no. 1:
Illegitimate child
appears unannounced.

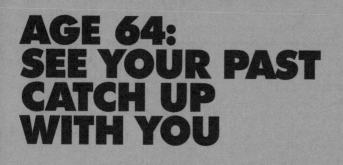

How to deal with it: At first deny all knowledge of them, particularly in front of your spouse, then come clean after being confronted with incontrovertible DNA evidence. Finally, embrace them as your own, unless they want money for drugs, in which case get them committed.

Crisis from your past no. 2:
A loved one you thought had
died appears unannounced.

How to deal with it: Peer at them confused for ten seconds, mumbling "But that's impossible...," then hug them crying to your bosom, and spend the next hour listening to their implausible explanation of how they swam to safety/landed on a haystack/ were bionically reconstituted by the government.

At some point in life, something you've done always comes back to haunt you. 64 is the most suitable age. You're nearly retired, but you're still young enough to deal with a crisis. Here are the main types of crisis you can expect.

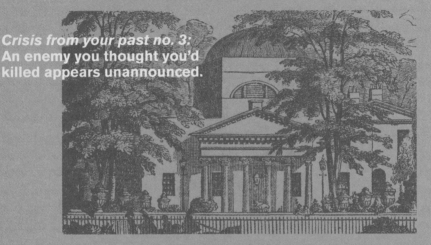

Crisis from your past no. 3:
An enemy you thought you'd
killed appears unannounced.

How to deal with it: Peer at them confused for ten seconds, mumbling "But that's impossible…," then notice the gun pointed at your heart. Let them tie you up as they tell you the story of how they survived, and what they're going to do to you now in revenge. Go straight to the instructions for age 86.

Crisis from your past no. 4:
Someone says something cryptic,
triggering your subliminal Soviet
sleeper-assassin programming.

How to deal with it: Let your eyes glaze over, fetch your two-piece sniper rifle, say good-bye robotically to your spouse of thirty years, and head off to Washington, D.C.

AGE 65: RETIRE AT LAST

Here is a guide to what they mean by this retirement gold watch, and what your response should be.

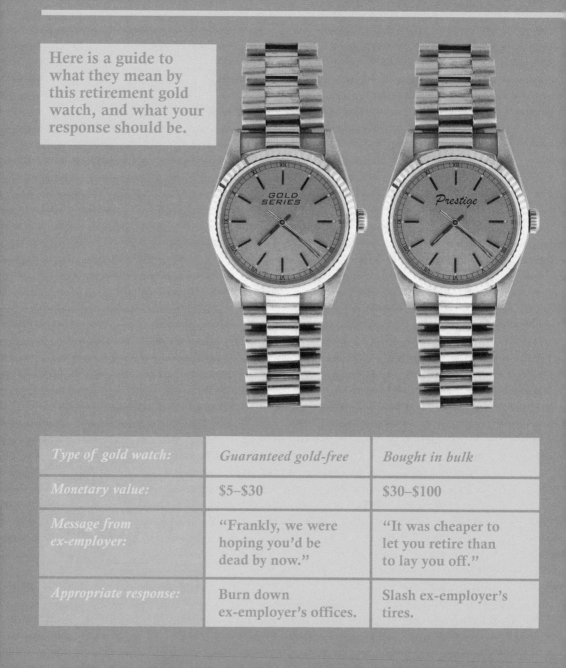

Type of gold watch:	Guaranteed gold-free	Bought in bulk
Monetary value:	$5–$30	$30–$100
Message from ex-employer:	"Frankly, we were hoping you'd be dead by now."	"It was cheaper to let you retire than to lay you off."
Appropriate response:	Burn down ex-employer's offices.	Slash ex-employer's tires.

Bravo! You have earned a well-deserved rest from the wage slavery that has blighted your existence. On this occasion, your ex-employer will reward you for a lifetime of service with a gold watch of some description.

Swiss	Rolex	Fake Rolex
$100–$300	$10,000–$50,000	$1–$25
"Thanks for your 40 years of hard work, good-bye now."	"You won't tell about that minor bookkeeping issue, will you?"	"We're about to go bust, and so is your pension plan."
Shake hands bitterly with ex-employer.	Shake hands happily with ex-employer.	Call FBI about "minor bookkeeping issue."

AGE 66:
GO ON A
CRUISE

Cruise follows retirement as surely as night follows day. You've been dreaming of it all these years: now is the time to sail around the Caribbean for six months in the company of your spouse, and other congenial types. Relax!

Rules to follow if the cruise goes wrong and you are stranded in a lifeboat with nothing to eat except each other:

1. Wait at least until the next mealtime before you start eating each other.
2. Make extra sure there's no other food lying in or around the lifeboat.
3. The captain gets eaten first, as punishment for sinking the boat.
4. Draw straws to find out who gets eaten next.
5. If no one remembered to bring the straws, the fattest person goes next.
6. In case of dispute, the fattest person is the one who denies it loudest.
7. Don't eat the person all at once. Eating one limb a day gives them some chance of survival. Their screams may also help alert rescuers.
8. Don't let them eat their own flesh, as that would be creepy, and probably poisonous.
9. Remember: the liver is very nutritious, but the lungs are pretty much inedible.
10. If it's your turn to be eaten, destroy this piece of paper and claim the rules have changed.

AGE 67: COMPOSE YOUR AUTOBIOGRAPHY

At 67, it is time to start passing on your experience to the younger generations. They will be grateful for your nuggets of hard-won wisdom, distilled from a lifetime of restless experimentation. Here are a few snappy titles that you may use freely; pick the one that suits your life most.

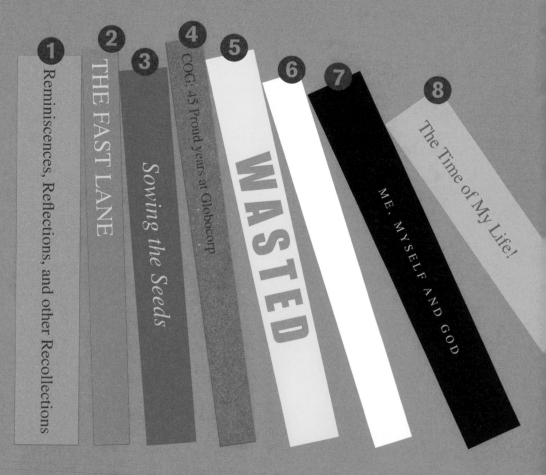

1. Reminiscences, Reflections, and other Recollections
2. THE FAST LANE
3. Sowing the Seeds
4. COG: 45 Proud years at Globocorp
5. WASTED
6.
7. ME, MYSELF AND GOD
8. The Time of My Life!

1. Boring life
Dedicate it to: "My family, friends and colleagues"

2. Eventful life
Dedicate it to: "Arnie, Paris, Tiger, Madonna, Woody, Keanu, Hillary, Kofi, Osama"

3. Family life
Dedicate it to: "Suzie, Charlie, Jeremy, Bradley, Sophie, Emily, Billy and Tommy"

4. Workaholic life
Dedicate it to: "Arthur H. Meckleburger III, the wisest Fortune 500 CEO who ever lived"

5. Drunken life
Dedicate it to: "My best buddy Jimmy Beam"

6. Failed life

7. Religious life
Dedicate it to: "Repentant Sinners"

8. Happy life
Dedicate it to: "Everyone I've ever met! You guys are great!"

AGE 68: MOVE TO FLORIDA

Don't get lost!

Try not to get separated from the flock. If you do, keep
an eye out for other lost seniors, and regroup for safety
against muggers and other predatory young people. Make
your way to the Sunshine State under cover of darkness,
using the stars as your compass. If all else fails, hijack a
Greyhound bus and get it to drive you straight to Tampa.

Once people reach a certain age, they instinctively head for Florida, much as ageing elephants head for their sacred graveyards. This year, you are ripe for migration. Here is a map that shows you the itinerary from wherever you currently reside.

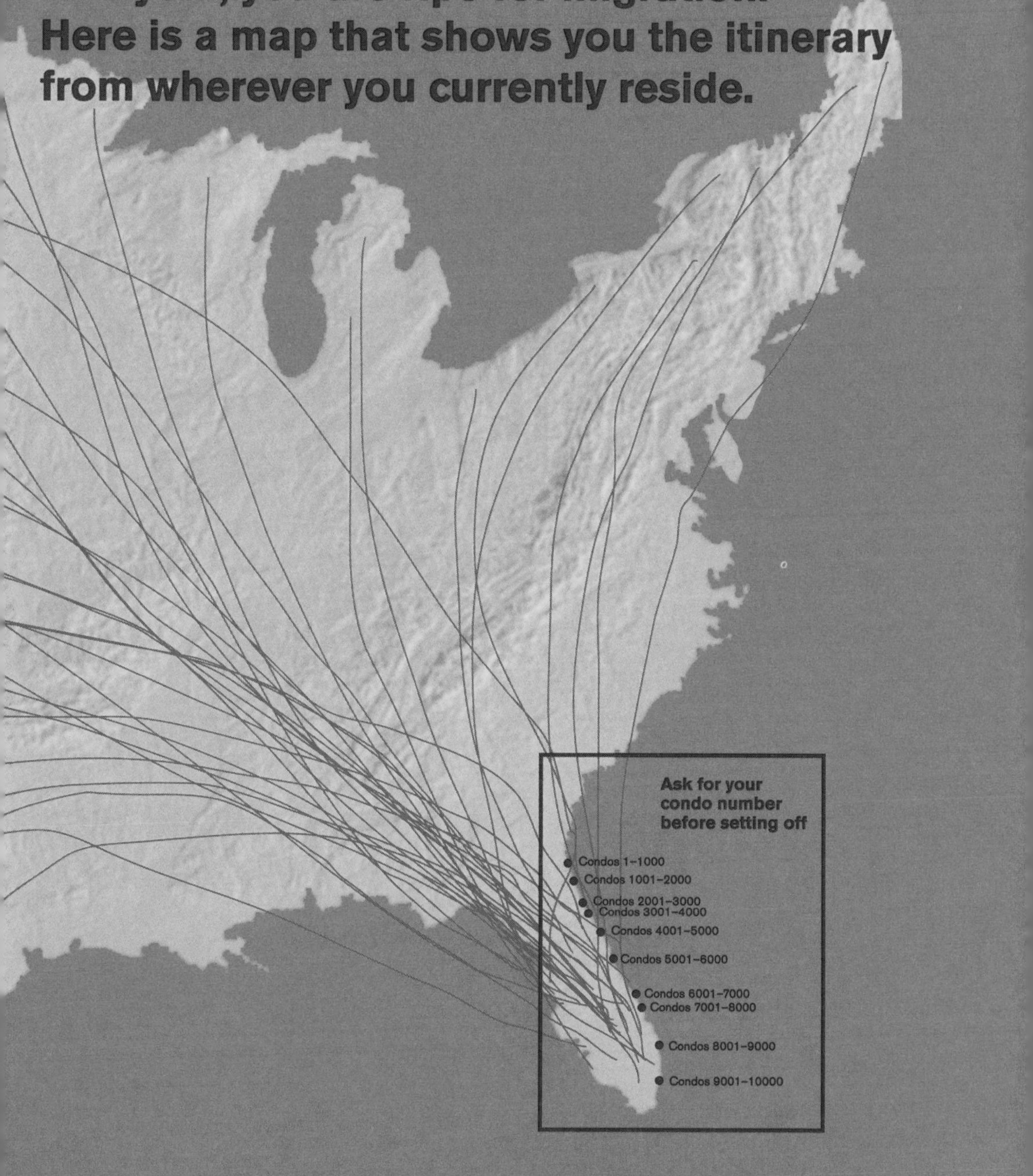

Ask for your condo number before setting off

- Condos 1–1000
- Condos 1001–2000
- Condos 2001–3000
- Condos 3001–4000
- Condos 4001–5000
- Condos 5001–6000
- Condos 6001–7000
- Condos 7001–8000
- Condos 8001–9000
- Condos 9001–10000

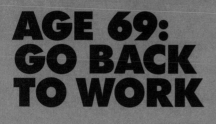

AGE 69: GO BACK TO WORK

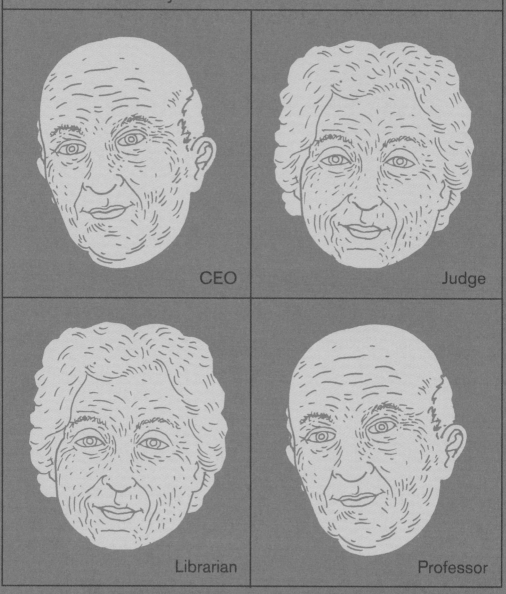

Jobs where the older you are the better:

CEO

Judge

Librarian

Professor

There's only so much fishing, golfing, gardening and coupon-clipping that a retiree can take. After a few years, you will realize how bored you are, and decide to go back to work. Be careful though: some jobs are better to go back to at 69 than others.

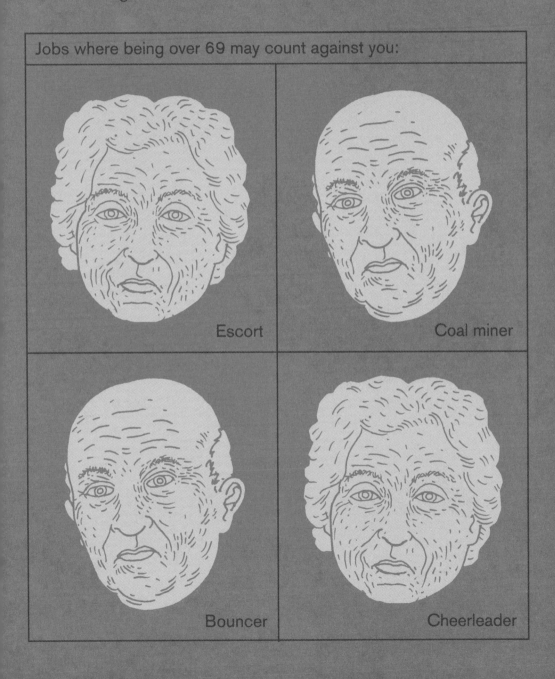

Jobs where being over 69 may count against you:

Escort

Coal miner

Bouncer

Cheerleader

AGE 70: JOIN THE ELDERLY

At 70, your status is no longer in doubt: you are now officially a member of that different species, the "elderly." Membership of the elderly comes with its pros and cons, but above all it requires you to conform to certain inescapable clichés. Tick them off as you go along.

CLICHÉ 1 ☐
Always claim to feel the cold.

CLICHÉ 2 ☐
Talk to other elderly people, even though you've never met them before.

CLICHÉ 3 ☐
Become invisible to anyone under 40.

CLICHÉ 4 ☐
Bake cookies, cakes, and other antiquated foodstuffs.

CLICHÉ 5 ☐
Keep your life savings under the mattress.

CLICHÉ 6 ☐
Preface every other remark with "When I was your age."

CLICHÉ 7 ☐
Dress mostly in beige and/or gray.

CLICHÉ 8 ☐
Put lining paper in your drawers.

CLICHÉ 9 ☐
Carry a cane of some description.

CLICHÉ 10 ☐
Be patronized by young people who think they'll never be old themselves.

AGE 71: SPOIL YOUR GRANDCHILDREN

If your offspring have reproduced on schedule, you should have a few bouncy grandkids to indulge by now. Spoiling grandchildren is a fiercely competitive sport, pitting you against their parents, as well as their other, lesser, grandparents. The goal is to become the prime focus of their lifelong affection. As in love and war, anything goes…

How to buy your grandchildren's lifelong affection
(cookies per visit)

1 COOKIE

2 COOKIES

3 COOKIES

4 COOKIES

5 COOKIES

| Grandchild will bounce on your knee for hours on end | Grandchild will give you a big kiss when you leave | Grandchild will make faces when kissed by rival grandparents | Grandchild will publicly declare they prefer you to their parents | Grandchild will mention you in wedding speech |

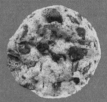

ENOUGH
COOKIES
TO MAKE YOU
THROW UP

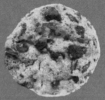

ENTIRE
COOKIE JAR

8 COOKIES

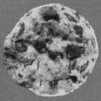

7 COOKIES

6 COOKIES

Grandchild will
name firstborn
after you

Grandchild
will cry
unconsolably
at your funeral

Grandchild
will visit your
grave every year
after you die

Grandchild
will give you
special chapter
in memoirs

Grandchild will
undergo years of therapy
to stop associating love
with cookies

AGE 72: RECORD YOUR MEMORIES WHILE YOU STILL CAN

Earliest memory

Age: 0

Details:..
....
....
....

Memory of bouncing on father's knee

Age: 3

Details:..
....
....
....

Memory of mother looking sad

Age: 4

Details:..
....
....
....

Memory of best school friend

Age: 5

Details:..
....
....
....

Memory of bullying

Age: 6

Details:..
....
....
....

Memory of being told the facts of life

Age: 7

Details:..
....
....
....

Memory of childhood Christmas

Age: 9

Details:..
....
....
....

Memory of crush on teacher

Age: 11

Details:..
....
....
....

Don't let old age rob you of your early years. At 72, there's still time to write down your memories before Alzheimer's or some equally foreign-sounding disease takes them away from you. Use the boxes provided.

Memory of first kiss — Age: 14

Details:..

Memory of first true love — Age: 17

Details:..

Memory of seeing the Eiffel Tower — Age: 23

Details:..

Memory of wedding day — Age: 28

Details:..

Memory of first child — Age: 30

Details:..

Memory of drunken car crash — Age: 37

Details:..

Memory of day divorce came through — Age: 46

Details:..

Memory of fighting war against the droids on Pluto (implanted) — Age: 49

Details:..

AGE 73: COUNT YOUR BLESSINGS

Prehistorical Human
(13,000 B.C.)

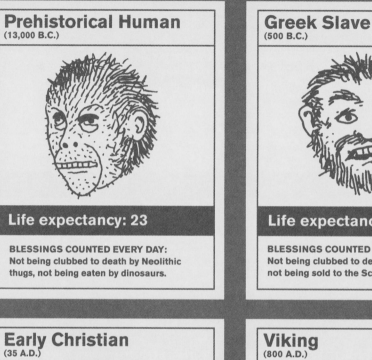

Life expectancy: 23

BLESSINGS COUNTED EVERY DAY:
Not being clubbed to death by Neolithic thugs, not being eaten by dinosaurs.

Greek Slave
(500 B.C.)

Life expectancy: 26

BLESSINGS COUNTED EVERY DAY:
Not being clubbed to death by slave-owner, not being sold to the Scythians.

Early Christian
(35 A.D.)

Life expectancy: 29

BLESSINGS COUNTED EVERY DAY:
Not being crucified,
not being fed to starving lions.

Viking
(800 A.D.)

Life expectancy: 32

BLESSINGS COUNTED EVERY DAY:
Not being pickaxed to death and having grog drunk out of one's skull by other Vikings.

In historical terms, you are incredibly lucky to be alive at this ripe old age; in times past, you would have been dead long ago. So count your blessings every day of this year. To help you focus, here are reminders of previous life expectancies you might have enjoyed.

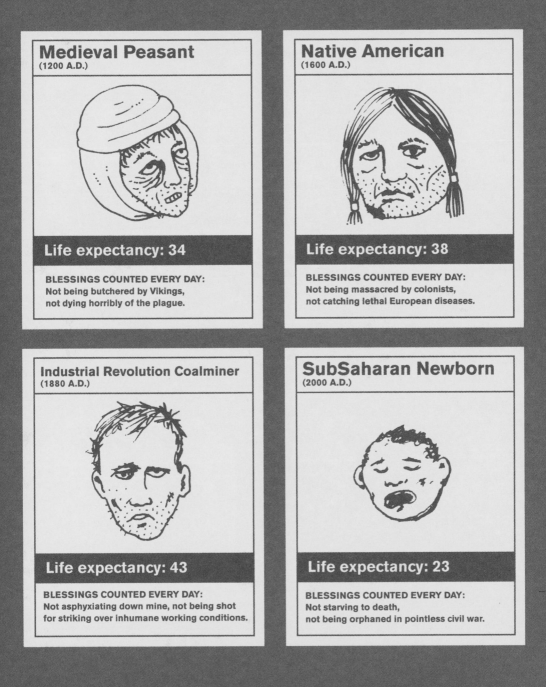

Medieval Peasant
(1200 A.D.)

Life expectancy: 34

BLESSINGS COUNTED EVERY DAY:
Not being butchered by Vikings,
not dying horribly of the plague.

Native American
(1600 A.D.)

Life expectancy: 38

BLESSINGS COUNTED EVERY DAY:
Not being massacred by colonists,
not catching lethal European diseases.

Industrial Revolution Coalminer
(1880 A.D.)

Life expectancy: 43

BLESSINGS COUNTED EVERY DAY:
Not asphyxiating down mine, not being shot
for striking over inhumane working conditions.

SubSaharan Newborn
(2000 A.D.)

Life expectancy: 23

BLESSINGS COUNTED EVERY DAY:
Not starving to death,
not being orphaned in pointless civil war.

AGE 74: AGE DISGRACEFULLY

One of the unexpected benefits of old age is that you are no longer required to act like a grown-up. If you behave outrageously, it's simply put down to senility and forgiven. Enterprising seniors get away with murder whenever they can; they realize it keeps them young.

SUPER MARKET

Do not go gentle into that good night.
Rage, rage against the dying of the light!

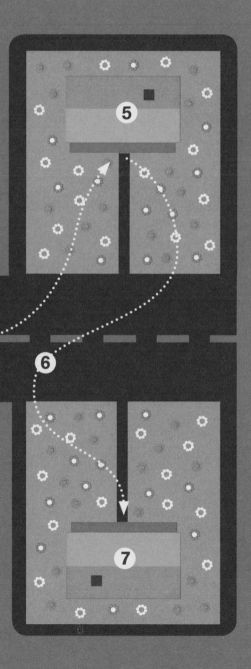

1) **DRIVING** Experienced seniors prefer to drive on the so-called wrong side of the road, where you get a better view of the oncoming traffic, and hence a better chance of dodging it.

2) **PARKING** At 74, you tend to drive a smaller car, which makes it easier to weave in and steal some suburban SUV-driving Mom's parking spot.

3) **CHATTING** Most people are reluctant to inflict violence on the elderly. The elderly know this, which is why they feel free to yell at most people, including protesting SUV-driving Moms. Shaking your fist is also common.

4) **SHOPPING** At 74, you know better than to pay full price for things. Or indeed to pay at all. Shoplifting is just the consumer version of absentmindedness.

5) **SOCIALIZING** If relatives won't visit you, you should drop in on them. Add to the guilt trip by repeating classic family feel-good lines such as "I wish I was dead."

6) **DRINKING** On the way home, help yourself to a few swigs from that bottle of malt you shoplifted earlier. It'll take the edge off your driving.

7) **RELAXING** As your hearing declines, you'll want to explore the limits of your TV's volume control. If you can still hear the neighbors banging on the wall, it's not loud enough.

AGE 75: HAVE A THREEQUARTERLIFE CRISIS

Frank Lloyd Wright (1867–1959)

Designed Guggenheim Museum at 80

Groundbreaking building I can still design:

....

....

....

....

Grandma Moses (1860–1961)

Sold her first painting at 80

World-famous paintings I can still paint:

....

....

....

....

The threequarterlife crisis is the logical counterpart to the quarterlife crisis (see "Age 25"). At 75, you should look in the rearview mirror of life and wonder if you measure up to posterity's standards. If not, don't worry: take heart from these individuals whose later achievements occurred well after 75. Plan your future exploits accordingly.

Winston Churchill (1874–1965)
Became British Prime Minister for the second time at 77

Major public position
I can still attain:

....

....

....

....

Johann Wolfgang von Goethe (1749–1832)
Finished writing his most famous tragedy, *Faust,* at 81

Masterpiece of Western
literature I can still write:

....

....

....

....

AGE 76:
REMARRY

Twinkle in eye

Laughter lines

No kids to take care of

Plenty of time on hands

Lifetime of sexual experience

76 is the perfect age to fall in love again. After your messy divorce at 46, you know what can go wrong in a relationship. You're free from family and work obligations. And you still have 24 years ahead of you! Here is what you should be looking for in a remarriage partner.

Understanding

No ticking biological clock

Patience

Comfortable with own body

No PMS

What if I'm still together with my original partner? This is highly unlikely, but at the very least renew your vows.

AGE 77: PREPLAN YOUR FUNERAL

I wish to be buried ☐

Coffin material:

Mahogany......☐	Walnut..........☐	Cherry............☐	Stainless steel.☐	Bronze...........☐	Copper...........☐	Titanium........☐

Coffin style:

Plain ☐   Tastefully decorated ☐   Kitsch ☐

Coffin brand:..

Cemetery:

No1 choice:..

No2 choice:..

No3 choice:..

Price range:

$100-$500 ☐

$500-$1,000 ☐

$1,000-$3000 ☐

$3,000-$10,000 ☐

$10,000+ ☐

Epitaph to be engraved on my tombstone:

"...

....

....

.... "

Music   Yes ☐ No ☐

Classical.................................☐

Rock..☐

Jazz...☐

Country/folk...........................☐

Hip-hop...................................☐

Specific request:.........................

....

....

....

....

Guests   Yes ☐ No ☐

Please invite the following:................

....

....

....

....

....

....

....

....

Please do not invite the following:

....

....

....

....

....

....

....

....

Well done! You have reached the average life expectancy of 77. Even though you probably still have many years to go, the odds are against you from now on. Be prepared: don't leave the details of your potential death to anyone else. Indicate your preferences below, and file these pages with your will.

I wish to be cremated ☐

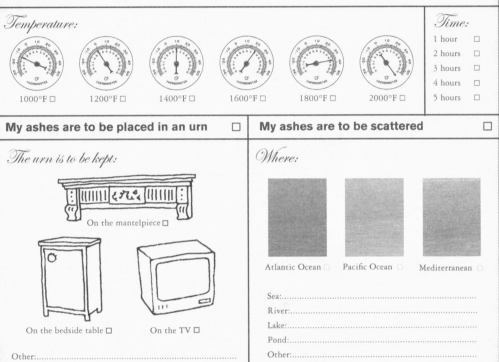

Temperature:

1000°F ☐ 1200°F ☐ 1400°F ☐ 1600°F ☐ 1800°F ☐ 2000°F ☐

Time:

1 hour ☐
2 hours ☐
3 hours ☐
4 hours ☐
5 hours ☐

My ashes are to be placed in an urn ☐

The urn is to be kept:

On the mantelpiece ☐

On the bedside table ☐   On the TV ☐

Other:...

My ashes are to be scattered ☐

Where:

Atlantic Ocean ☐   Pacific Ocean ☐   Mediterranean ☐

Sea:...
River:...
Lake:..
Pond:..
Other:...

Priest   Yes ☐ No ☐

Dear Priest,
Please claim that I am now:
in Heaven.............................. ☐
in Hell................................ ☐
in Purgatory........................... ☐
LENGTH OF SERVICE
2 hours ☐ 1 hour ☐ 20 minutes ☐
PALLBEARERS
Number: 2 ☐ 4 ☐ 6 ☐ 8 ☐ 10 ☐

Flowers   Yes ☐ No ☐

Type: ....
....
....
....
....
Known allergies:...................
....
....
....
....
....

Overall mood

Somber.................................... ☐
Festive...................................☐
Relieved.................................. ☐
Other:....................................
....

CRYING
Yes....................................... ☐
No.. ☐
Widow and children only....... ☐

AGE 78: REUNITE YOUR ROCK BAND

These days, it is perfectly acceptable to rock well into your golden years, as countless ageing stars have proven. Try and locate the other members of your teenage band using the note boxes below, and reform for a Reunion Tour.

BAND MEMBERS*

VOCALS
Name:..
Last seen:...
Last known address:...
....
Still alive? Yes ■ No ■   Health status: Mobile ■ Not mobile ■
Current address:..
....
Interested in reuniting? Yes ■ No ■ No memory of the band ■

GUITAR
Name:..
Last seen:...
Last known address:...
....
Still alive? Yes ■ No ■   Health status: Mobile ■ Not mobile ■
Current address:..
....
Interested in reuniting? Yes ■ No ■ No memory of the band ■

BASS
Name:..
Last seen:...
Last known address:...
....
Still alive? Yes ■ No ■   Health status: Mobile ■ Not mobile ■
Current address:..
....
Interested in reuniting? Yes ■ No ■ No memory of the band ■

DRUMS
Name:..
Last seen:...
Last known address:...
....
Still alive? Yes ■ No ■   Health status: Mobile ■ Not mobile ■
Current address:..
....
Interested in reuniting? Yes ■ No ■ No memory of the band ■

KEYBOARD
Name:..
Last seen:...
Last known address:...
....
Still alive? Yes ■ No ■   Health status: Mobile ■ Not mobile ■
Current address:..
....
Interested in reuniting? Yes ■ No ■ No memory of the band ■

TAMBOURINE
Name:..
Last seen:...
Last known address:...
....
Still alive? Yes ■ No ■   Health status: Mobile ■ Not mobile ■
Current address:..
....
Interested in reuniting? Yes ■ No ■ No memory of the band ■

TRIANGLE
Name:..
Last seen:...
Last known address:...
....
Still alive? Yes ■ No ■   Health status: Mobile ■ Not mobile ■
Current address:..
....
Interested in reuniting? Yes ■ No ■ No memory of the band ■

OTHER
Name:..
Last seen:...
Last known address:...
....
Still alive? Yes ■ No ■   Health status: Mobile ■ Not mobile ■
Current address:..
....
Interested in reuniting? Yes ■ No ■ No memory of the band ■

*cf Age 16

AGE 79: TALK ABOUT THE WAR

World War I

Date: 1914-1918
Location: World
Cause: Evil inbred-royal plans
Severity: 9/10
Outcome: Triumphant victory of freedom and democracy

Plausible war story: *"I'd been in the trench for six months when they finally gave the signal. A tremendous great cheer erupted, we all went over the top, and the damn jerries mowed everyone down, except me."*

World War II

Date: 1939-1945
Location: World
Cause: Evil Nazi world-domination plans
Severity: 8/10
Outcome: Triumphant victory of freedom and democracy

Plausible war story: *"We jumped off the craft onto Omaha Beach. Within a few seconds, shells started exploding all around us. We ran like hell. Then the kraut snipers spotted us. No one in my unit survived, except me."*

Korea

Date: 1950-1953
Location: Korean peninsula
Cause: Evil commie world-domination plans
Severity: 4/10
Outcome: Semi-triumphant victory of freedom and democracy

Plausible war story: *"We'd been marching through the mountains toward Chisan for five days along with 3 RAR. As we reached the Pukhan River, the gooks opened up with 60mm mortars and wiped out the whole goddamn platoon, except me."*

Vietnam

Date: 1961-1973
Location: Southeast Asia
Cause: Evil commie world-domination plans
Severity: 6/10
Outcome: Ignominious US withdrawal

Plausible war story: *"We could smell Charlie. We knew he was near, waiting for us to trip up. So we called in airstrikes to bomb the hell out of the closest berns. But air con got it wrong and called it on us. No one found cover in time, except me."*

By 79, you will have been expected to partake in a war or two, and to be able and willing to discuss them at great length. But don't worry if you missed out—here is a handy guide to some recent conflicts that you may claim to have played a part in. Just try not to lie to anyone who was actually there.

Women: one of the hard-won victories of the last 100 years has been women's right to die horribly for their country as well. So feel free to regale youngsters with your tales of heroic derring-do, just like your menfolk. Although for the more old-fashioned wars, you may be more credible if you claim to have driven ambulances, nursed the injured, run the home front and suchlike.

Cold War

Date: 1945-1989
Location: World
Cause: Evil commie world-domination plans
Severity: 2/10
Outcome: Triumphant victory of freedom and democracy

Plausible war story: *"My cover had been blown. I needed to get out of Bratislava, and fast. Our local agents hid me in a secret compartment on a coal barge bound for Vienna. Alas, we were boarded by the KGB, who tortured everyone to death, except me."*

Civil War

Date: 1861-1865
Location: USA
Cause: Evil Confederate slave-driving plans
Severity: 7/10
Outcome: Triumphant victory of freedom and democracy

Plausible war story: *"We were camped out by the Potomac, fall of 1863, after a ten-day march. I'd wandered into town to requisition some food from the natives. By the time I got back, the Rebels had ambushed my squad. Not a soul survived, except me."*

Gulf War I

Date: 1991
Location: Kuwait, Iraq
Cause: Evil Saddam Hussein plans
Severity: 2/10
Outcome: Triumphant victory of freedom and democracy

Plausible war story: *"I was flying a Stealth bomber back from taking out government targets in Baghdad. We got hit by a SAM and had to eject. We landed in the desert in the middle of the night and got separated. No one made it back to base, except me."*

Gulf War II

Date: 2003-
Location: Iraq
Cause: Evil "axis of evil" plans
Severity: 5/10
Outcome: N/A (Either "Triumphant victory of freedom and democracy" or "Ignominious US withdrawal")

Plausible war story: *N/A (You may only start telling war stories after hostilities are formally declared at an end)*

AGE 80: RISK IT ALL

George Bush Sr. celebrating his 80th birthday with a parachute jump. If George can do it, SO CAN YOU!

If you have reached the age of 80 in one piece, you have nothing much to lose. Go all out and risk your neck on some adrenaline-pumping extreme sport that will give you something to boast about on judgment day. Yee-ha!

CALL NOW TO BOOK!
Parachuting
703-836-3495

CALL NOW TO BOOK!
Paragliding
719-632-8300

CALL NOW TO BOOK!
Bungee jumping
503-520-0303

CALL NOW TO BOOK!
Base jumping
707-793-2297

CALL NOW TO BOOK!
Street luge
723-250-4175

AGE 81: FIGHT BACK AGAINST AGEISM

Boycott the capitalist economic system until ads feature more seniors!

Discredit prominent teen idols!

As you reach 81, you will realize that ageism permeates our society from top to bottom. From commercials that only feature under-35s to websites with unreadably small type, everything is geared toward the young. Peaceful options have long been exhausted. To fight for your rights, you must join the underground struggle.

Sabotage
the factories of
anti-ageing cream
manufacturers!

Rob banks
to fund
Medicare!

Firebomb
cosmetic
surgery
clinics!

Kidnap TV execs
until their schedules
stop skewing
toward the 18-34
demographic!

"Old age will only be respected if it fights for itself." (Cicero)

AGE 82: START A COLLECTION OF SOMETHING POINTLESS

At 82, you will form the urge to take up a new hobby, usually collecting. Your family will encourage you in this, as it makes gift buying much more straightforward. Here are some suitably harmless things to collect, although you may pick your own–the dottier the better.

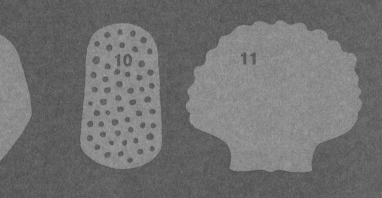

Dottiness rating		
1	Stamps	1/5
2	Porcelain dolls	2/5
3	Buttons	2/5
4	Eggcups	4/5
5	Ceramic hedgehogs	4/5
6	Matchbooks	3/5
7	Angels	3/5
8	Coasters	2/5
9	Coins	1/5
10	Thimbles	4/5
11	Shells	2/5
12	Toy tractors	5/5
13	Swim caps	5/5

AGE 83: DISINHERIT YOUR UNDESERVING RELATIVES

Disinheriting your spouse

This isn't quite as easy as it should be, at least not in all states. Spouses are generally entitled to a good chunk of your assets. But you can at least try.

Disinheriting your children

Kids are disturbingly easy to disinherit. The only catch is that you have to make your intention explicit, otherwise the courts will assume you forgot them accidentally.

SPOUSE

I, ..., being of sound mind, hereby disinherit my spouse.
Spouse's name:...
Reason for disinheritance:.......................................
Signed:........................... Dated:...............
Witnessed:...

SON no. 1

I, ..., being of sound mind, hereby disinherit my son.
Child's name:...
Reason for disinheritance:.......................................
Signed:........................... Dated:...............
Witnessed:...

SPOUSE no. 2

I, ..., being of sound mind, hereby disinherit my second spouse.
Spouse's name:...
Reason for disinheritance:.......................................
Signed:........................... Dated:...............
Witnessed:...

SON no. 2

I, ..., being of sound mind, hereby disinherit my son.
Child's name:...
Reason for disinheritance:.......................................
Signed:........................... Dated:...............
Witnessed:...

SPOUSE no. 3

I, ..., being of sound mind, hereby disinherit my third spouse.
Spouse's name:...
Reason for disinheritance:.......................................
Signed:........................... Dated:...............
Witnessed:...

DAUGHTER no. 1

I, ..., being of sound mind, hereby disinherit my daughter.
Child's name:...
Reason for disinheritance:.......................................
Signed:........................... Dated:...............
Witnessed:...

SPOUSE no. 4

I, ..., being of sound mind, hereby disinherit my fourth spouse.
Spouse's name:...
Reason for disinheritance:.......................................
Signed:........................... Dated:...............
Witnessed:...

DAUGHTER no. 2

I, ..., being of sound mind, hereby disinherit my daughter.
Child's name:...
Reason for disinheritance:.......................................
Signed:........................... Dated:...............
Witnessed:...

One of the unsung pleasures of old age is the ability to disinherit any family member who hasn't been sufficiently attentive to you. However, you must make sure they can't contest your will. Use the forms below to put everything in writing and thus help avoid any unseemly legal battles after your death.

Disinheriting your grandchildren

Disinheriting your grandkids is generally considered fairly mean, but if the little brats have done something to deserve it, why not?

Disinheriting your minor relatives

Minor relatives are harmless fun to disinherit. In fact, it is practically compulsory to do so. Pick the ones who've been sniffing around your money most blatantly.

GRANDSON no. 1
I, ..., being of sound mind, hereby disinherit my grandson.
Grandchild's name:...
Reason for disinheritance:.......................................
Signed:.............................. Dated:...............
Witnessed:..

DISTANT RELATIVE no. 1
I, ..., being of sound mind, hereby disinherit my distant relative.
Relative's name:...
Reason for disinheritance:.......................................
Signed:.............................. Dated:...............
Witnessed:..

GRANDSON no. 2
I, ..., being of sound mind, hereby disinherit my grandson.
Grandchild's name:...
Reason for disinheritance:.......................................
Signed:.............................. Dated:...............
Witnessed:..

DISTANT RELATIVE no. 2
I, ..., being of sound mind, hereby disinherit my distant relative.
Relative's name:...
Reason for disinheritance:.......................................
Signed:.............................. Dated:...............
Witnessed:..

GRANDDAUGHTER no. 1
I, ..., being of sound mind, hereby disinherit my granddaughter.
Grandchild's name:...
Reason for disinheritance:.......................................
Signed:.............................. Dated:...............
Witnessed:..

GIVING EVERYTHING TO A LONG-LOST RELATIVE

Another good trick is to give everything to a relative you've never met. In conjunction with disinheriting the others, you will ensure your will is talked about for years after your passing.

GRANDDAUGHTER no. 2
I, ..., being of sound mind, hereby disinherit my granddaughter.
Grandchild's name:...
Reason for disinheritance:.......................................
Signed:.............................. Dated:...............
Witnessed:..

LONG-LOST RELATIVE
I, ..., being of sound mind, hereby bequeath everything I own to my long-lost relative.
Relative's name (if known):....................................
Reason for surprise inheritance:............................
Signed:.............................. Dated:...............
Witnessed:..

AGE 84: DISCUSS NOTHING BUT YOUR DISEASES

TOPIC: THE ECONOMY

"I couldn't agree more, I'm very worried about the budget deficit too, it's almost as high as my blood pressure these days, 170/90, my doc says he's never seen anything like it."

TOPIC: WAR

"Yes, I've heard there's been terrible suffering in Sudan since the invasion, and to tell you the truth, I know how they must be feeling, why, my hip is simply killing me."

TOPIC: LOVE

"Well yes, it's marvelous that he's proposed and you've said yes dear, I remember when I married your father, he was so handsome, now of course I can't see him much, my eyesight is going."

TOPIC: ART

"No, I didn't see that film, although I saw his previous one, in the days before my back pain when I could still sit in a cinema. It really is a curse, you know."

By 84, various aches and pains will have started to dominate your daily life. They are the inevitable companions of old age, and often the only remedy will be to talk about them incessantly. Here is how to divert any topic of conversation toward the issue of your health.

TOPIC: POLITICS

"You're right, her candidacy will never unite the center ground, it's obvious, it'll lead the party to a slow and painful decline, a bit like my hemorrhoids."

TOPIC: SCIENCE

"Sending a mission to Mars would push back the boundaries of human endeavor, I agree, but when are they going to do something about my swollen ankles?"

TOPIC: HISTORY

"Yes, Napoleon was a terrible dictator. He lived in the nineteenth century, didn't he? Diabetes then was a death sentence. Now they say it's easier to manage. Personally I don't think so."

TOPIC: CRIME

"45 victims chopped up and eaten over ten years? I hope he gets the death penalty, or failing that, gout. People don't realize but it truly is torture, my friend."

AGE 85: WANDER THE WORLD IN SEARCH OF ENLIGHTENMENT

In the Hindu worldview, we progress through four life stages, or ashrama: student, householder, retirement and finally sannyasin. Sannyasin is where the individual renounces all ties and possessions and becomes a hermit, wandering the world in search of cosmic wisdom. This is an eminently sensible course of action, and 85 is the proper age at which to embark upon it. Say good-bye to your loved ones and friends, clothe yourself in a warm blanket, and set off on your one-year quest. Good luck.

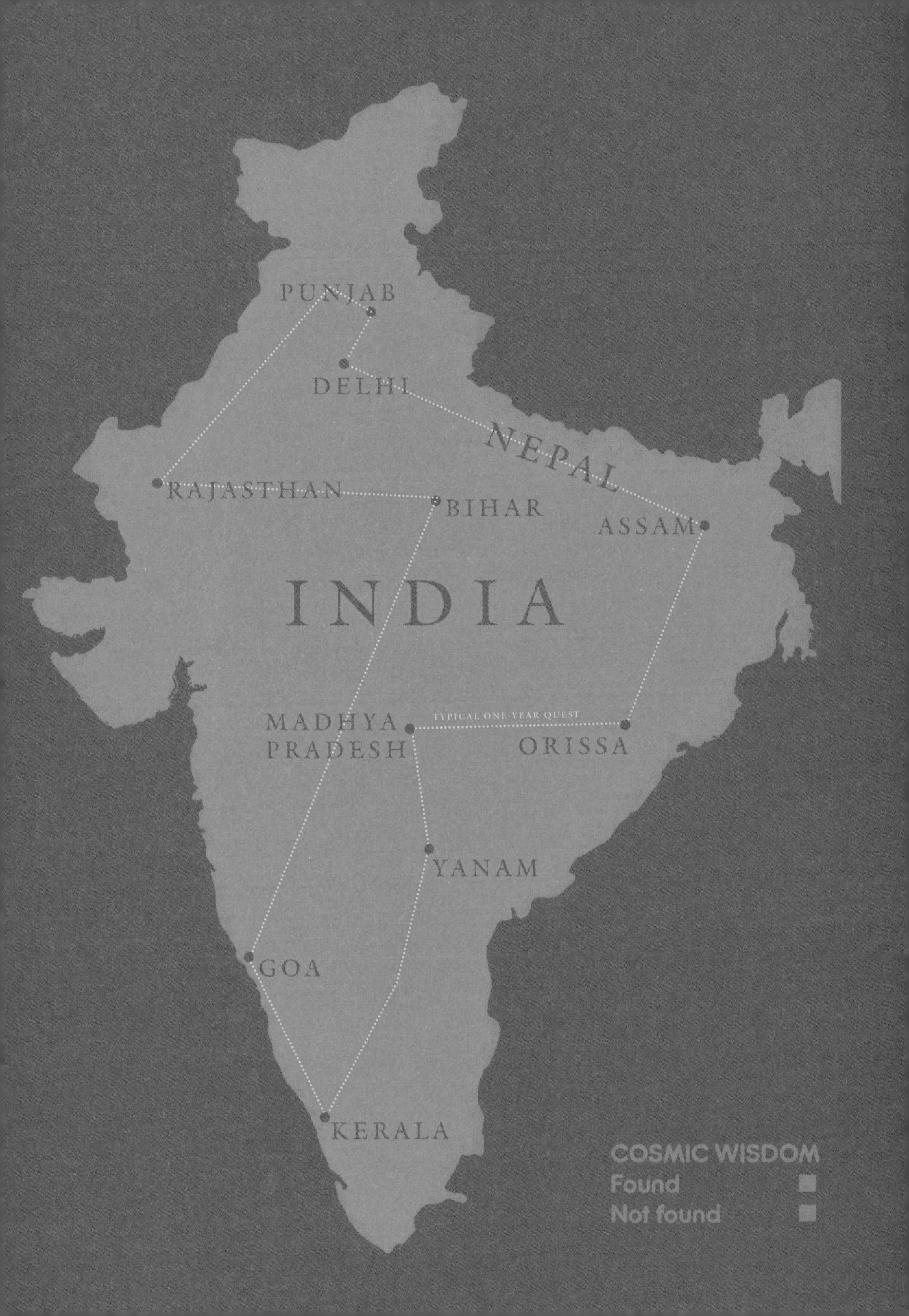

PUNJAB

DELHI

NEPAL

RAJASTHAN

BIHAR

ASSAM

INDIA

MADHYA
PRADESH

TYPICAL ONE YEAR QUEST

ORISSA

YANAM

GOA

KERALA

COSMIC WISDOM
Found
Not found

AGE 86:
MAKE PEACE
WITH GOD

At 86, you should start
thinking about the afterlife.
However dissolute your life may have
been, there is still time to make amends.
Pray forgiveness to God, and remind
him of some of your good deeds so that
you may sit by his side in heaven.

"Dear God,
As I approach my final years,
I realize that
I have ignored your teachings
throughout my life,
and that in countless ways
I have failed you.
I am not worthy to be
accepted by you, and do
not deserve to spend
eternity by your side.
You are my master and
I beg you for forgiveness.
I believe in you wholly and
place my soul in your hands.
Thank you God."

My top 3 Good Deeds (please consider these on Judgment Day)

1...

2...

3...

AGE 87: MAKE PEACE WITH SATAN TOO

It doesn't hurt to cover all the bases:
now that you've made peace with God,
make peace with Satan as well, just
in case he's in charge. Use the following
prayer, and list your worst sins, so that
Satan may look upon you favorably
and spare you the hellfire.

"Dear Satan,
As I approach my final years,
I realize that
I have ignored your teachings
throughout my life,
and that in countless ways
I have failed you.
I am not worthy to be
accepted by you, and do
not deserve to spend
eternity by your side.
You are my master and
I beg you for forgiveness.
I believe in you wholly and
place my soul in your hands.
Thank you Satan."

My top 3 Bad Deeds (please consider these on Judgment Day)

1...

2...

3...

AGE 88:
RUN FOR
POPE

In Memoriam

There are some things you can only do when you've reached a certain age. Running for pope is definitely one of them—being ancient is part of the job description. Becoming pope does involve considerable effort and tenacity, particularly if you're a woman.* But the benefits are non-negligible: apartment in Rome, pope-mobile, adulation, autocratic leadership of a major historical faith. Here is how to go about it.

1) PUT YOUR NAME DOWN.
In theory, you have to be a cardinal in order to become pope. Historically, however, this has not always been the case: lay people have been elected to the papacy before, and only then ordained as priests and bishops. This is your chance. Write to the Vatican to announce your candidacy for the job, and be sure to remind them of the historical precedent.

2) LOBBY THE CARDINALS.
Once you have publicly joined the race, the cardinals will take a keen interest in you. They elect the pope by secret ballot, so are open to flattery, bribery and threats, just like any normal politicians. Focus on the positive side of your candidacy, however, by pointing out how at 88 you really look the part.

3) WAIT FOR A VACANCY.
This can take a while, but sadly there isn't much you can do to speed things up. Assassination is still an option, but could get you excommunicated, which would be a major obstacle to your papal ambitions. But don't worry too much; one of the benefits of electing ageing popes is that they're bound to meet their Father before too long.

4) GET ELECTED!
Once the pope is dead, the college of cardinals gathers in a conclave in the Sistine Chapel, and cannot leave until the new pope is elected. After your lobbying, you should be on the shortlist. If you're elected, take over spiritual authority for millions worldwide. If not, at least you won't have spent your 89th year vegetating in front of the TV.

*FEMALE CANDIDATES Contrary to official accounts, there has been a female pope. In the 850s, Pope Joan was elected, although she was disguised as a man. She was uncovered as she mounted a horse, her waters broke, and she gave birth to a son. According to some chroniclers, she was immediately stoned to death. Nevertheless, a precedent was set. Ladies, don't hold back: the time is ripe for a popess.

AGE 89: LIST YOUR REGRETS

Common Regret: I never climbed Mt. Kilimanjaro/ Mt. Everest/Mt. Fuji.

Solution: Call a specialist travel agent and book your trip. **Wilderness Travel (1-800-368-2794)**

Common Regret: I never kissed that boy/girl I had a crush on in high school.

Solution: Locate them and find out if they have regrets about you. **ICDA Investigations, Inc. (1-800-491-4232)**

As you reach near the end of your voyage through life, you will develop regrets. At 89, however, there's still time to do something about them. Here are a few common regrets, along with simple solutions to implement immediately.

Common Regret:
I never skinny-dipped
in the Pacific Ocean.

Solution: Book your flight
and skinny-dip within a week.
Hawaiian Airlines
(1-800-367-5320)

Common Regret:
I never tried LSD
in the sixties.

Solution: Locate your nearest drug
dealer and buy a couple of tabs.
DEA (202-307-1000)

AGE 90: TALK TO NONHUMANS

Talking to cats
"Hello kitty kitty, that's a good puddy tat meoooowwww!"

Talking to dogs
"Hey, Pongo, bark once if you think I should invest in this stock. OK!!! Attaboy..."

Talking to pigeons
"Come here my creatures, come to Mommy, ahahahahaha..."

Talking to goldfish
"Helluva boring show tonight, dontcha think, Jaws?"

By 90, it is your prerogative to talk to anyone or anything without expecting an actual answer. You've heard it all by now, and have probably come to the conclusion that your side of the conversation is more interesting anyway.

Talking to plants

"You're a thirsty little plant, aren't you? Yes you are, vain to deny it!"

Talking to the kettle

"Look! She's flirting with the mailman again, what a hussy! Did you see that?"

Talking to your dearly departed spouse

"Oh darling, you haven't touched your dinner…What am I to do with you?"

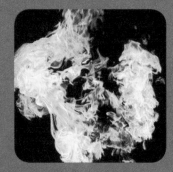

Talking to yourself

"Well I never, somebody's left the iron on all night again!"

AGE 91: REPLACE A LIMB

After a long and eventful life, your body will naturally start to fall apart. Fortunately, you live in an era where modern science can provide replacement parts. Decide which ones you require below and request them from your local surgeon. Note: As this book is written for future generations as well as the current one, we have included anticipated developments, along with an estimate of when they might become available.

	Indications:	Available:	Procedure:
1. Hip replacement	Pain caused by osteoarthritis and rheumatoid arthritis.	Now.	Hip joint is exposed and hip socket is cleared out and replaced.
2. Knee replacement	Pain or restricted function of the knee joint.	Now.	Removal of arthritic joints and replacement with metal components.
3. Artificial heart	Imminent heart failure.	Now.	Excision of patient's ventricles, and transplantation in seven-hour operation under general anesthetic.
4. Eye replacement	Total or partial blindness.	2009 (est.)	Computer chip is implanted at the back of the retina linked directly to the brain.
5. Bionic arm	Loss of limb through accident.	2014 (est.)	Arm nerve cells attached to electrodes that control mechanical prosthesis.
6. Cyborg colon	Colon eaten away by alien spores from 2022 meteorite.	2037 (est.)	Six-foot-long cyborg colon inserted rectally under local anesthetic.
7. Artificial memory	Replacement of failing memory with all the information on the Internet, along with 256MB of free storage for any personal data.	2049 (est.)	Built inside the brain by self-destructing nanosurgeonbots.

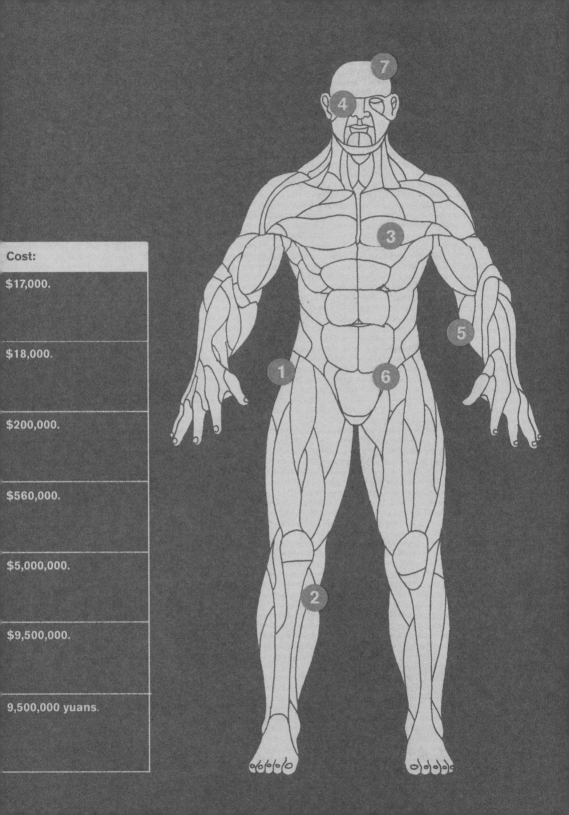

Cost:

$17,000.

$18,000.

$200,000.

$560,000.

$5,000,000.

$9,500,000.

9,500,000 yuans.

AGE 92: FRIGHTEN YOUR GREAT-GRAND-CHILDREN

"The gremlins stole my teeth one moonless night when I made the mistake of sleeping with my mouth open."

"When I was your age, the king used to flog little children who didn't brush their teeth before bedtime."

"My castle was on top of the tallest volcano in the world. One day I came back from shopping and BOOM up it went."

"The dragon breathed on me with such bad breath that my skin turned wrinkled overnight."

At 92, you are a figure of legend to your
great-grandchildren, a quasi-medieval beast
who might as well be 600 years old.
Kindle this myth, and make a lasting imprint
on their young minds with some tall tales that
will chill them to the bone.

"These sweets will make your brains
boil and ooze out of your earholes,
but by golly they're worth it!"

"Your Daddy and Mommy
were born in eggs, I saw it
with mine own eyes."

"Of all my brothers and sisters, I was
the only one that escaped being sucked
to death like a lollipop by the Big Bad
Witch—and her evil dwarf lover."

"I've eaten many many juicy
young children, but you're family
so I would never eat you!"

AGE 93: SPREAD YOUR WISDOM

A) NON-WESTERN CULTURES:
At 93, you are now considered to be at the peak of your wisdom, a fount of knowledge and experience, a venerable elder who naturally assumes leadership of the tribe. The younger members of your community will respectfully consult you on matters of importance. Use your unquestionable sagacity to steer them on the right course.

B) WESTERN CULTURE:
Try spreading your wisdom, just don't expect anyone to listen.

AGE 94: ENSURE YOUR PLACE IN HISTORY

1. ENGAGING STORYTELLING
Students these days have limited attention spans. Make your piece of history as gripping as any Hollywood movie!

2. STUNNING VISUALS
Include some exciting pictures from your younger, more photogenic days.

3. HOMEWORK TIPS
Focusing homework on the "humorous" side of the subject makes it more likely it'll get done!

Brian Mason, *American hero*

Chapter 4
A Difficult Decade

On October 24th, 2003, Brian Mason's life went downhill, when he was arrested for driving under the influence of alcohol and released on bail after a night in Bedford County Police Station, Pennsylvania. Despite having double the legal limit of alcohol in his blood, Mason testified on the scene that the driver behind him was at fault:

"Baaam! Some guy drove straight into the back of my new Camry! Well, I don't mind telling you, I was ticked off! I got out and gave him a piece of my mind and no mistake"

That driver was Louise Morgan, a 36-year-old mother of two, whom Mason proceeded to berate for failing to anticipate his sudden braking. Morgan subsequently sued and obtained a restraining order forbidding Mason to go within 300ft of her and her children. Sadly for Mason, this was merely the beginning of his troubles. The police investigation determined that Mason had become inebriated at the Fairview Motel, where he had shared a room with Tricia Gonzalez, an exotic dancer. His wife Marcia Mason, herself four months pregnant, petitioned for divorce and returned to her mother's in Baltimore, leaving this note: "I never want to see you again, you sad, sad, little man. How dare you do this to me. If you ever attempt to contact me again directly, or see my child, I will take you down. Goodbye." Although the historical evidence becomes sketchy, we know that at this point, Mason decided to turn to heroin. His descent

"Spring of '99: surfing in Maui! Woo-hoo!"

"List ten things that were particularly unappealing about Brian's college roommate."

1...................................
2...................................
3...................................
4...................................
5...................................
6...................................
7...................................
8...................................
9...................................
10..................................

By 94, you are naturally concerned with your legacy. The simplest way to guarantee your place in the history books is to write to their publishers directly, outlining your achievements. But to help them pick you over others, make sure your submission fits in with their editorial style.

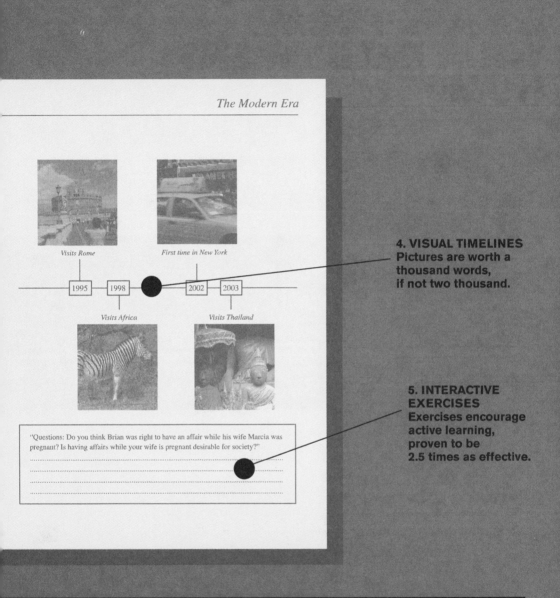

The Modern Era

Visits Rome

First time in New York

| 1995 | 1998 | ● | 2002 | 2003 |

Visits Africa

Visits Thailand

"Questions: Do you think Brian was right to have an affair while his wife Marcia was pregnant? Is having affairs while your wife is pregnant desirable for society?"

4. VISUAL TIMELINES
Pictures are worth a thousand words, if not two thousand.

5. INTERACTIVE EXERCISES
Exercises encourage active learning, proven to be 2.5 times as effective.

Send your requests to secure a place in history to the Social Studies departments of these leading textbook publishers:
PEARSON PRENTICE HALL, One Lake Street, Upper Saddle River, NJ 07458
HOLT, RINEHART AND WINSTON, 10801 North Mopac Expy, Building 3, Austin, TX 78759
HARCOURT, INC. 6277 Sea Harbor Drive, Orlando, FL 32887
MCDOUGAL LITTELL, A Houghton Mifflin Company, 1900 S. Batavia, Geneva, IL 60134
GLENCOE MCGRAW-HILL, 2 Penn Plaza, New York, NY 10121-0101

AGE 95: ESCAPE FROM YOUR RETIREMENT HOME

A. TUNNEL ESCAPE:
Dig at night, using whatever sharp implement is available, e.g., a teaspoon or a letter opener. Get rid of the earth from the tunnel by dispersing it in the camp's vegetable patch. N.B. Only attempt Plan A if you live on the ground floor.

B. HELICOPTER ESCAPE:
Contact a friend with a helicopter. Ask them to hover at a predetermined time, lower a rope, and whisk you away to freedom. If you require a walker, this option may prove impractical.

You haven't survived this long to spend your twilight years rotting away in some glorified prison camp in an overmedicated coma. Make a break for it, using one of these tried-and-trusted escape plans.

C . OVER THE WALL ESCAPE:
Non-electrified: scale the wall with an extension ladder, taking care not to fracture your bad knee as you make the twelve-foot drop on the other side. Electrified: make sure that you wear rubber gloves, and check your pacemaker is fitted with a fuse.

D. DOUBLE-BLUFF ESCAPE:
Just try strolling out the front gate, smiling confidently at the guards. If stopped, claim you've been pardoned. If this fails to convince, grab the guard's tazer and take him hostage.

You're free at last! Now live on the run for the next five years.

AGE 96: SPEND WHATEVER YOU HAVE LEFT

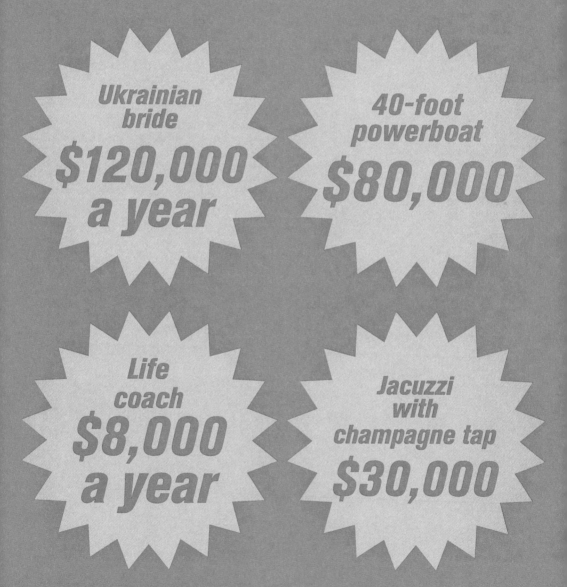

Ukrainian bride
$120,000 a year

40-foot powerboat
$80,000

Life coach
$8,000 a year

Jacuzzi with champagne tap
$30,000

You can't take it with you, so enjoy your cash while you can. At 96, you're allowed to be irresponsible: treat yourself to anything you've ever wanted, and preferably things that will infuriate your heirs. Here are some suitable 96-year-old purchases that will run your bank balance down to nil.

Personal flotation tank
$12,000

Week in Monte Carlo
$70,000

Italian toyboy
$115,000 a year

Sculpted marble bust of yourself
$15,000

AGE 97: UNCOVER THE MEANING OF LIFE

By now, you should have a fair idea what it's all been about. The authors are conducting a poll of our 97-year-old readers to try to get a statistically accurate answer. We will post the results online at www.thiswebsitewillchangeyourlife.com.

Benrik Poll

I, ...,

having lived to 97, reckon the purpose of life is:

1. "To become rich"... ☐
2. "To do unto others as you would have them do unto you" ☐
3. "To know thyself".. ☐
4. "To help others".. ☐
5. "To make the world a better place".................................... ☐
6. "To enjoy yourself while you can"....................................... ☐
7. "To find beauty"... ☐
8. "To find God"... ☐
9. "To become God"... ☐
10. "To impose your will on everyone else"............................ ☐
11. "To cease striving".. ☐
12. There is no meaning of life.. ☐
Other (specify):..

....

....

....

Send to: Benrik Limited "Meaning of life" Poll, C/o Waxman Literary Agency, 80 Fifth Avenue, Suite 1101, New York, NY 10011, USA.

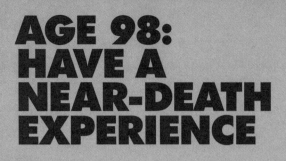

AGE 98: HAVE A NEAR-DEATH EXPERIENCE

You are indisputably nearing the twilight of your life now, so this is the correct time to have one of those fabled "near-death experiences" and see what all the fuss is about. Simply fall on your head to provoke a concussion, and enjoy the show!*

Common near-death experiences and how to react to them as you regain consciousness.

CASE 1: BRIGHT WHITE LIGHTS
Significance: Bright white lights are tediously common, and usually mean you're waking up in the middle of surgery.
How to react: Gesture frantically for more anesthetic.

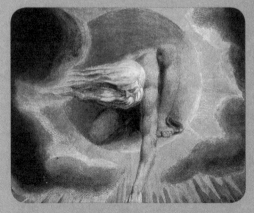

CASE 2: VISION OF GOD
Significance: God may sometimes appear briefly. Try to notice if he is smiling or scowling at you.
How to react: If God was scowling, hurry up and make amends.

CASE 3: FILM OF YOUR LIFE
Significance: Watching the film of your life is fairly routine in near-death experiences.
How to react: If you find it boring, you only have yourself to blame.

CASE 4: ATOMIC CHAOS
Significance: Your TV set needs adjusting.
How to react: Call repairman.

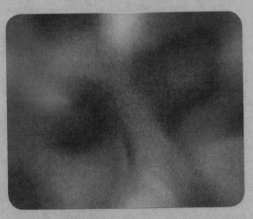

CASE 5: SLOW-MOVING BLOBS OF COLOR
Significance: Nurse spotted you falling on your head deliberately, and has put you on powerful tranquillizers.
How to react: Relax…

CASE 6: DARKNESS
Significance: Utter darkness could mean you are being afforded a precious glimpse of infinity.
Or it could mean that you are in fact truly dead.
How to react: N/A

AGE 99: LIVE FOR THE MOMENT

IF YOU'VE MADE IT TO 99, YOU MAY PUT THIS BOOK DOWN, STOP PLANNING, AND ENJOY THE REST OF YOUR LIFE.

AGE 100: UNDERGO CRYOGENIC FREEZING

CONGRATULATIONS! You have lived for an entire century, through wars, plagues, and other similarly nasty events. Now it's time to quit while you're ahead, and preserve your brain for future generations to revive.

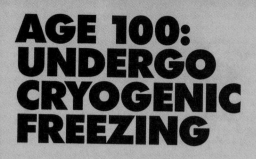

1. Contact a lab
Most of the cryogenic facilities are in California. Some will only freeze you once you're actually dead, so you may need to shop around.

2. *Make an appointment*
Say good-bye to loved ones. You may only
see them again when they're 100 themselves.

3. *Have your heart stopped*
It doesn't hurt. At least there
haven't been any complaints.

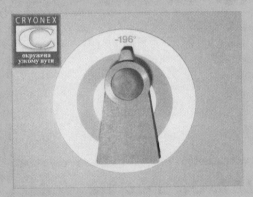

4. *Freeze*
Your body is submerged in liquid
nitrogen, which at –196°C will keep you
nice and fresh for the next few decades.

5. *Undergo reanimation*
Once future generations have fine-tuned the
process, they'll microwave you back to life.

HOW TO PREVENT FUTURE GENERATIONS FROM REVIVING YOU AS PART OF A REALITY TV SHOW.

As soon as you are revived, ask to see a lawyer.
If you are revived in what seems to be a suspicious
form, e.g., as a talking poodle, or a transsexual alien,
assume you are on TV, and claim a fee.
Do not be fooled by talk of millions of dollars;
by then, millions will probably be worthless.

LIFE SUMMARY

Once you have reached the end of your life, briefly sum up the highlights here.

YOUR 15 MINUTES OF FAME

When:................................

Where:...............................

Details:..............................

....

GOAL IN LIFE:

....

....

....

....

Achieved ☐   Not achieved ☐

YOUTHFUL ILLUSIONS

1.......................................

2.......................................

3.......................................

Buried here:.........................

YOUTHFUL INDISCRETIONS

1.......................................

2.......................................

3.......................................

Put behind you? Yes ☐   No ☐

WERE YOU EVER EMPLOYEE OF THE MONTH?

Month:...............................

Year:..................................

Company:............................

LESSON YOU'VE LEARNED:

(e.g. "Violence never solved anything")

....

....

....

....

HAVE YOU LED A LIFE OF QUIET DESPERATION?

Yes   ☐

No   ☐

Noisy desperation   ☐

DID YOU FULFIL YOUR EARLY PROMISE?

Yes   ☐

No   ☐

When did you realize you would never fulfil your early promise?..................

**BEST YEAR OF
YOUR LIFE:**

....

**BEST FRIEND
OF YOUR LIFE:**

....

**HOLIDAY OF
A LIFETIME:**

....

**LIFETIME
ACHIEVEMENT:**

....

**TOP NEWS EVENT
IN YOUR LIFETIME:**

....

**MEAL OF
YOUR LIFE:**

....

**LOVE OF
YOUR LIFE:**

....

**WHAT YOU WOULD
DO IF YOU COULD DO
IT ALL OVER AGAIN:**

....
....
....

PHOTO ALBUM OF MY LIFE

Affix photos of yourself as you grow older.

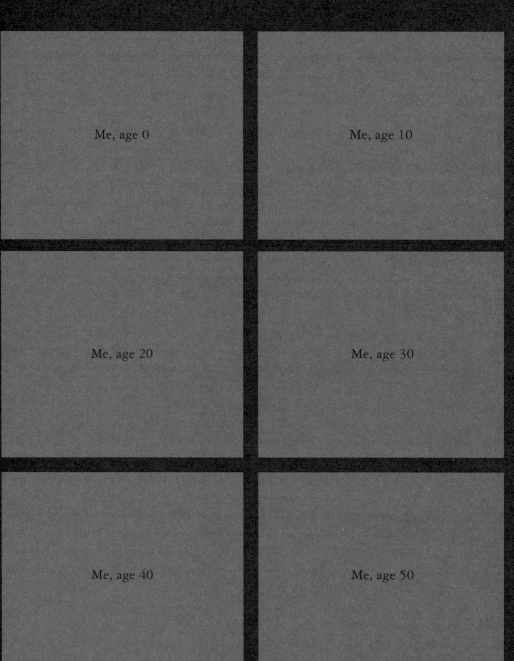

Me, age 0

Me, age 10

Me, age 20

Me, age 30

Me, age 40

Me, age 50

Me, age 60

Me, age 70

Me, age 80

Me, age 90

Me, age 100

All-time favorite
photo of me

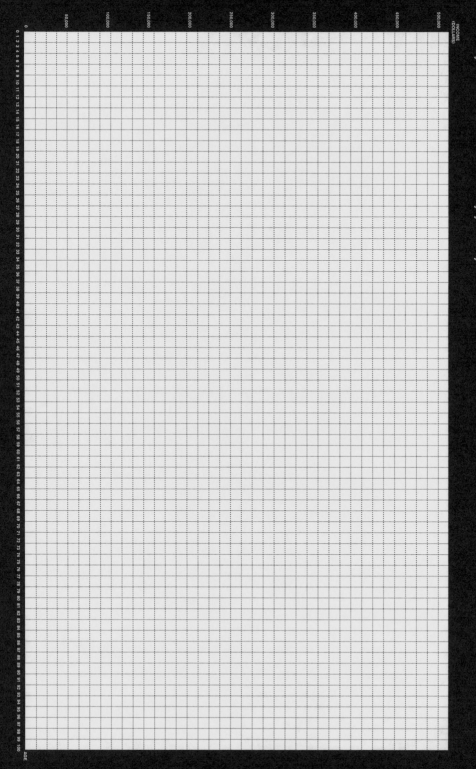

LIFE MONEY CHART

Plot your exact income for every year of your life.

INCOME
(DOLLARS)

AGE

LIFE DIET CHART

Mark your exact weight for every year of your life.

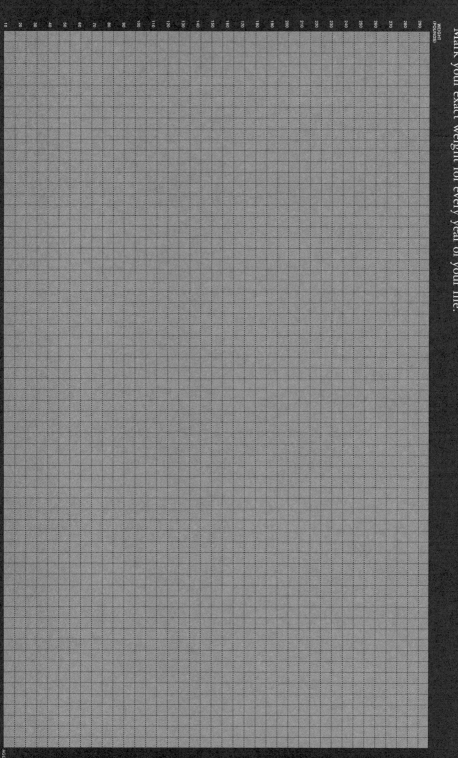

WEIGHT
(POUNDS)

10 20 30 40 50 60 70 80 90 100 110 120 130 140 150 160 170 180 190 200 210 220 230 240 250 260 270 280 290

AGE

Benrik are grateful for the help and support of the following people, whose combined age is 3898. Extra special thanks to:
Nikki Lindman and Billy Waqar for assisting Benrik, Erik Enberg for copy on ages 50, 55 and 62, Marthe Nagengast for
illustrations on ages 70, 84, 92. The usual special thanks to: Kathy Peach, Lana & Anton Delehag, Trena Keating, Emily Haynes,
Fabiana Leme, Melissa Jacoby, Lily Kosner, Marie Coolman and all at Plume, Simon Trewin, Claire Gill, Maria Dawson,
Scott Waxman, Farley Chase, Andy Moreno, Emil Lanne, Shailesh Gor, Mark Cole, Matthew Eade, Robert Saville, Mark Waites,
Matt Clark, Piers North and all at Mother, Jens, Erik and all at Saturday, all at Poke, Trevor Franklin, Marc Valli, Aidan Onn,
Sarah Aplin, Hannah Sherman, Emma Beddard, Sarah Bagner, Dominic Goodrum, Stuart Phillips, Ben, Kim and Lola Ruddy, Stephanie
Molloy, Roman Marszalek, Richard Prue Alex & Elizabeth Carey, Aunt, Katy, Antony and Talulla, Stefanie Charlotte and
Tommy Drews, Gaby Teresa and Rafael Vinader, Sarah Woodruff, Emma Lowe, Jan Lyness, Sally Evans, Alan Payne, Rebecca Bland,
Bernard Sue and John Peach, Kenneth & Anna-Lena Delehag & Lovisa & Hjalmar & Elin Delehag, hela släkten.

www.thiswebsitewillchangeyourlife.com
All illustrations, photography, design and typography by Benrik, except as follows.
Where the work is not property and copyright of the authors, all attempts have been made by the authors to contact correct
copyright holders. The authors would like to gratefully thank for permission to include the following within this edition:
Benrik official portrait © Piers North; illustrations ages 70, 84, 92 © Marthe Nagengast (www.marthenagengast.com); photography
ages 0 © Ray Massey/Getty Images, 9 © Nicola Tree/Getty Images, 13 © Daly & Newton/Getty Images, 26 © Norma Zuniga/Getty
Images, 29 island © Tony May/Getty Images, 29 living room © Photonica/Getty Images, 37 lawyers © Jim Arbogast/Getty Images,
53 left © Tom King/Getty Images, 53 right © Mike Powell/Getty Images, 57 man top left © Wide Group/Getty Images, 57 man bottom
left © Alan Powdrill/Getty Images, 57 man top right © Patryce Bak/Getty Images, 57 woman top left © Marcus Luconi/Getty Images,
57 woman top right © Jason Todd/Getty Images, 57 woman bottom left © Kurt Hutton/Getty Images, 76 left © Martin Barraud/
Getty Images, 76 right © Siri Stafford/Getty Images, 88 © Franco Origlia/Getty Images, 93 © Angelo Cavalli/Getty Images, 99
© Philip Lee Harvey/Getty Images, 100 top right © Lambert/Getty Images, 100 bottom right © Terry Vine/Getty Images; photography
ages 29, 42, 43 (house) © John Henley/Corbis, 48 left © Underwood & Underwood/Corbis, 48 right © Bettmann/Corbis, 57 punk rocker
© Ronnie Kaufman/Corbis, 57 nun © Norbert Schaefer/Corbis, 66 Tom & Dee Ann McCarthy/Corbis, 78 © Andrew Gombert/epa/Corbis,
80 © Jeff Mitchell/Reuters/Corbis; age 90 (dog) © Jackson S; age 56 © Lana Ivanyukhina; age 74 "Do not go..." © Dylan Thomas.
If there is further enquiry, please contact the authors c/o PFD, Drury House, 34-43 Russell St, London WC2B 5HA, UK.

PLUME
Published by the Penguin Group
Penguin Group (USA) Inc., 375 Hudson Street, New York, New York 10014, U.S.A.
Penguin Group (Canada), 10 Alcorn Avenue, Toronto, Ontario, Canada M4V 3B2 (a division of Pearson Penguin Canada Inc.)
Penguin Books Ltd, 80 Strand, London WC2R 0RL, England
Penguin Ireland, 25 St Stephen's Green, Dublin 2, Ireland (a division of Penguin Books Ltd)
Penguin Group (Australia), 250 Camberwell Road, Camberwell, Victoria 3124, Australia (a division of Pearson Australia Group Pty Ltd)
Penguin Books India Pvt Ltd, 11 Community Centre, Panchsheel Park, New Delhi, 110 017, India
Penguin Books (NZ), Cnr Airborne and Rosedale Roads, Albany, Auckland, New Zealand (a division of Pearson New Zealand Ltd)
Penguin Books (South Africa) (Pty) Ltd, 24 Sturdee Avenue, Rosebank, Johannesburg 2196, South Africa
Penguin Books Ltd, Registered Offices: 80 Strand, London WC2R 0RL, England

Published by Plume, a member of Penguin Group (USA) Inc. First Plume Printing, November 2006

1 3 5 7 9 10 8 6 4 2

**Don't go through life on your own!
Join other Benrik followers on
www.thiswebsitewillchangeyourlife.com!**

Young Tommy Drews has kindly agreed to follow this book year by year for the rest of his life.
Good luck with it, Tommy!